Endor

For almost forty years, couples have said that the scriptural principles taught in the *Married for Life* course are analogous to building a home. Some have even drawn homes with principles depicted in the foundation, doors, windows, etc. While those discussions and illustrations were intriguing, we always felt there was more to what the Holy Spirit was saying. *The Marital Castle* captures the reality that God is not just building a house, but a fortress designed to protect marriage and family.

The journey through the Castle is led by the Holy Spirit, beginning with the intimacy and safety of the Inner Keep, through the Great Dining Hall where abiding with Jesus gives sustenance and life to the family, into the Marital Armory where our armor and the weapons of our warfare are at the ready, and into the War Room where battle strategies are revealed and weapons are designated. *The Marital Castle* reveals God's plan for marriage and family, and the sustaining life and protection that He provides to keep us and our family victorious against enemy attack. It is the most graphic picture of what God is building through *Married for Life* that we have ever seen.

We have no doubt that this book has been commissioned by the Lord for such a time as this. Today, when so many marriages are under attack, every married couple needs to learn how to live in the fullness of their Marital Castle. We pray that marriages and families around the world will be supernaturally transformed through this anointed message.
-Mike and Marilyn Phillipps

The Marital Castle will challenge your heart, beliefs, and prior misconceptions on God's true design for marriage and relationships. It is rich with revelation that has been undoubtedly saturated with God's light and presence. Julian possess a gift to communicate truth with vulnerability, authenticity, and sincerity. Whether you're building the foundation of your new marriage, or renovating an established covenant, the tools outlined in *The Marital Castle* will empower you to open your eyes, put on your amour, and defend your relationship against imminent attacks.
-Cameron and Madeleine Speed

Finally, a voice that cries out and tells the truth to this generation that your marriage is precious and worth saving! So many couples are living in secret pain, struggling with decisions that will have tragic consequences; feeling and believing the same lies that the author felt.

I can't thank Stephanie and Julian enough for being so transparent and sharing their true life-story with all of us. The revelations contained within the pages of this book have the power to transform your life, rescue your family, rebuild your relationships, and strengthen your marriage.

As with the Word of God, the principles must be acted upon to be successful. Like Jesus said in Matthew 7:24-27, we must be doers of the Word, and not hearers only, in order for our Marital Castle to stand strong and be able to withstand the hellish attacks that seek to destroy our one-flesh marriages and our families.

As you read, please allow the Holy Spirit to challenge your heart and reveal to you that your home can be victorious.

-Frank C. Menhart, Jr.
Senior Pastor, Blainesburg Bible Church, Brownsville, PA

The Marital Castle is a remarkable view of what God's plan for marriage should be. It vividly depicts so many scriptures that support the message needed to be heard by all married couples who need more than the survival mode in their marriage. If more couples could practice the art of protecting their castle with the tools shared within this book, the divorce rate would definitely drop drastically. Great testimony of how God never gives up on us, no matter where we are in life.

-Rick and Helen Cofer

The Marital Castle is helpful for singles and/or married individuals, regardless of the condition of their marriage. There are basic (yet profound) principles on salvation in Christ, and how the enemy can divert someone from their God-given path— as well as specific strategies, rooted in biblically-sound teaching, to prevent problems and improve, save, or turn around a hopeless marriage. These principles, when combined with faith, perseverance, and- most importantly- the Holy Spirit, will defeat the enemy.

-Dr. Tammy Pooler

The Marital Castle is an amazing insight into what God, The Son, and the Holy Spirit can do in our marital lives if we ask and submit to Him.

Combining reading this book with participating in *Married for Life* groups is truly a must for anyone that wants to experience the true one-flesh relationship that God intended for us to have.

Thank you, Julian and Stephanie, for your obedience to His calling!
-Rodney Jones

As a woman married for twenty-five years, and a participant in the Married for Life ministry, I believe this book will save thousands of marriages. Julian and Stephanie's willingness to be so transparent with their difficulties and triumphs allows the reader to see that no marriage is too badly damaged that the Lord cannot heal. Time spent reading this book will unleash a blessing over any marriage.
-Michelle Jones

We overcome by the blood of the Lamb and the word of our testimony. Julian weaves his testimony throughout the principles God showed him, making it easy to put the principles into context and apply to my own life. What a wonderful story of God's redeeming power!
-Mark

[*The Marital Castle*] is not only an amazing testimony of the power of God to reconcile and restore a marriage, but also full of strong, Biblical guidelines on how to protect and preserve your marriage. The author is transparent in sharing their journey through difficult marital troubles...but praise God for the example of restoration, even in sight of divorce court!

The Marital Castle is a powerful book because of its reliance on the Word of God. It will inspire you to worship, pray, work on your marriage, believe for miracles, and fall in love again with our God who is the cornerstone of our Marital Castle! Great book!
-Pastors Mike and Pat Brantley
Crescent Springs Church of God, Crescent Springs, KY

The Marital Castle

Why You Should Stay Married and How to Strengthen Your Fortifications

"Till Death Do You Part"

Julian Silas Adkins, Jr.
Stephanie Adkins

Title: The Marital Castle

Subtitle: Why You Should Stay Married and How to Strengthen Your Fortifications "Till Death Do You Part"

Author: Julian Silas Adkins Jr.
Co-Author: Stephanie Adkins
Editor: Laura Ohlman
Cover Art by: Amanda Welch

Published by: Amazon.com
ISBN: 9781076652829
www.amazon.com

All rights reserved. No part of this book may be reproduced or transmitted in any form or by any means, electronic or mechanical, including photocopying, recording, or by any information storage and retrieval system, without written permission from the author, except for the inclusion of brief quotations in a review, except as provided by United States of America copyright law.
Copyright © 2019 by Julian Adkins
The Marital Castle, First Edition, October 2019
Published in the United States of America

Unless otherwise noted, all Scripture quotations are from the New International Version of the Holy Bible. Copyright © 1973, 1978, 1984, International Bible Society. Used by permission.

Scripture quotations marked NKJV are from the New King James version of the Holy Bible. Copyright © 1979, 1980, 1982 by Thomas Nelson, INC., publishers. Used by permission.

Scripture quotations marked AMP are from the Amplified Bible. Old Testament copyright © 1965, 1958, 1987, by the Lockman Foundation. Used by Permission.

Scripture quotations marked NLT are taken from the Holy Bible, New Living Translation, Copyright © 1996, 2004, 2007 by Tyndale House Foundation. Used by permission of Tyndale House Publishers, Inc., Carol Stream, Illinois 60188.

The Library of Congress has catalogued the hardcover edition as follows:
Adkins, Jr., Julian Silas, Adkins, Stephanie
The Marital Castle: Why You Should Stay Married and How to Strengthen Your Fortifications "Till Death Do You Part"/Julian Silas Adkins, Jr., Stephanie Adkins-1st ed ISBN: 9781076652829 (Paperback)
1. Engagement 2. Love 3. Self-help 4. Marriage 5. Divorce 6. Newlywed 7. Christian

Dedication

This book is dedicated to my wife, Stephanie. You have been the "glue" that has kept us all together. Through all the times we struggled, and the times we didn't, you have been the cornerstone of our family. Thank you for your love and dedication in praying for our relationship, marriage, and family. Thank you for forgiving me. Your love has made me real, and I love you!

To my children, thank you for forgiveness and for giving me a second chance. This second chance will not be taken for granted. I love you all from the bottom of my heart, and I promise I will not let you down again.

I also want to say thanks to our *Married for Life* coaches, Rodney and Michelle, and Rick and Helen. Thank you for praying for us before you ever knew us. I know you put in countless hours of prayer on our behalf.

To God, my heavenly Father, thank You for opening Your arms to me and allowing me to return home to You. Thank You, my Lord and Savior, for forgiveness, for loving me, and for not keeping a record of my wrongdoings. Thank You for searching for me in the shadows and dark places. Thank You for leaving the ninety-nine to find me. Thank You for rescuing me and not allowing the enemy to keep me. Thank You, Holy Spirit, for showing me so much about where I was and how I got there. Thank You for providing insight and a clear picture of the institution of marriage. Thank you for guiding me through this book.

Table of Contents

PREFACE 10
Chapter 1 Calm Before the Storm 12
    Carried Away from the Marital Castle 20
Chapter 2 Leaving the 99 38
    God's Pursuit of the Captive 43
    Divorce Court: Take One 51
    Divorce Court: Take Two 56
Chapter 3 The Prodigal Husband 68
Chapter 4 The First Step is Obedience 78
Chapter 5 Marital Foundations 92
    Personal Spiritual Foundations 98
Chapter 6 Matters of the Heart 109
    The Inner Keep 109
    Repentance 114
    Forgiveness 122
    Farming Your Relationships 128
Chapter 7 The Castellum Keep 137
    Honesty 141
    Trust 144
    Physical Intimacy 150
    Love-The way Jesus Loves His Church 158
        One Flesh: This is a Profound Mystery 161
        Shiddukhin: A Mutual Covenant 163
        Erusin: The Betrothal 166

- Nissuin: The Marriage 169
- The Marriage Supper of the Lamb 172
- Chapter 8 The Great Dining Hall 185
  - John 6:53-58 192
  - The Bread of Life Explained 192
- Chapter 9 The Marital Armory 195
  - Spiritual Gifts, Armor, Weapons, and Enemy 198
    - Armor of God 198
    - Spiritual Gifts 204
    - Spiritual Weapons 215
    - The War-Room 225
    - The Enemy Briefing 228
    - Godly Strategies and Tactics 256
    - Our Spiritual Victories 264
- Chapter 10 Fortifications and Defenses 281
- Annexes of the Marital Castle 289
  - Stephanie's Faith Vision 289
  - Spiritual Warfare Scriptures 293
  - Prayer Study: When Jesus Prayed 298
  - 2=1 International 302
  - About Our Ministry-The Marital Castle 305
  - Bibliography of Sources 307

PREFACE

If your marriage was a castle, how fortified would you say it is? When did you last climb the tower and survey your lands? Looking out over the ramparts and feeling the warm breeze in your face, is all quiet on the horizon?

Perhaps even as you read this, the enemy is advancing against your castle. Has he developed a deceptive strategy against you? What if he has been secretly digging a tunnel for years to break through your marital foundation and trespass against your marriage? Should you sound the alarm and call your banners of war?

Maybe the attack on your castle has already begun and you're in a battle for your marriage— or your life. Is everything you've worked for falling to pieces around you?

Voices around you have differing opinions regarding your next steps, but what is God saying about the state of your marriage?

Does the God of the universe— the Alpha and the Omega, the One True God, have time for your crumbling castle? Does He even care? The answer is **YES!**

He has known you since before you were born. His plans for you are explained in Jeremiah 1:5 and 29:11. He has memorized every detail about you and knows the number of hairs on your head (Matthew 10:30 and Psalm 139). Did you know He has assigned unique gifts to you

(Romans 12:6-8)? He can help in your time of crisis, if you only let Him.

This book was written on Biblical principles and Scriptures, along with guidance from the Holy Spirit— who was my driving force. Although I may have written this book, Stephanie lived what is written on these pages. She, along with God, is just as much an author of our story as I am.

Whether you are engaged, married, or divorced, I pray you give God a chance. My wife and I leaned on Him when there was no hope to be found. He not only turned our marriage around, He saved it and me.

Take a moment and listen. Step away from social media and all the peripheral noise. Be still (Psalm 46:10), open the eyes of your heart, and listen to what God has to say about you and your relationship. Let the Holy Spirit speak to you. He is the same yesterday, today, and forever.

He never changes. His word stands firm. He will never misguide you.

Chapter 1

Calm Before the Storm

I found myself at 3,000 feet above the ground. It was the spring of 2015, and the colors were vividly bright. I could feel the heat of the sun shining on my face and burning on my skin, especially my forearms. Everything was a blur and all noise was muted. I wasn't sure where I was or what I was doing. Some questions flashed through my mind. *How did I get here? Where am I? Where am I going?*

Below me, I could see palm trees and various other subtropical vegetation, as well as dark-colored lakes for miles. I'd had aerial views like this before during my twenty-plus years in the US Army while performing duties as a paratrooper. Many times, I stood in the door of a C-130 gunship with the brisk wind against me, looking ahead for the drop zone with great anticipation of jumping and getting myself out and away from a perfectly good airplane.

Views of homes, trees, roads, bodies of water, fields of grass, automobiles, and sometimes people were a familiar sight from high elevations. I'd had to ensure I had my bearings and solid orientation when I exited the plane. At high altitudes, I had the advantage of quickly identifying East and West, and distinctive landmarks like bodies of water or other noticeable terrain. It wouldn't be long before I was on the ground and lose that advantage.

However, this time I wasn't wearing a parachute, or even a reserve. I didn't have a combat helmet on and wasn't wearing the familiar green camouflage uniform I wore on other airborne operations. I could see I was wearing a short-sleeved shirt and perhaps even shorts; nonetheless, I still wasn't sure what was happening. I asked myself, *am I drugged*?

My orientation and location were still a mystery. I could still see tall palm trees, lakes everywhere, and even expressways below me. White sand beaches ran parallel to me. I turned my head to the left and could see the beautiful blue ocean extending beyond the horizon. To my right was more ocean, and I noticed that it was emerald green. As far as I could see in front of me, there was nothing but tropical vegetation.

Wait! I noticed muffled sounds now. My vision became clearer and my hearing was being restored. Under my feet was glass, which allowed me to see the view below. I realized I had no flight instruments, and my altitude estimation was only that, an estimate. I made an assessment that I was west of Jacksonville, Florida, flying south.

The expressways must have been I-95 heading south and I-10 heading west. My feet were engaging with foot pedals, of which I clearly understood to be part of some helicopter. The rapid swoosh-swoosh-swoosh sound became louder as the helicopter's blades turned rapidly to support the machine in flight.

My hand was on the control stick as I looked around the small cockpit I could see the throttle on my left set at 50%. The helicopter was agile— just a little twist of the cyclic stick and it would change direction. There was a constant, but faint, high-pitch whine coming from a turboshaft engine behind me. I felt the helicopter's unique vibrations in my bones. From my air assault missions while in the Army, I recognized the cyclic compressive force vibration coming from the engines— although this helicopter was much smoother compared to Army aircraft.

I now realized I was wearing sound-proof headphones, which contributed to the muffled noises. On occasion I could hear radio traffic from other aircraft. This was my first time piloting a helicopter and I found it easy. I had previously used flight simulator software which made it feel real, but never to this extent. Flying a helicopter using the simulator was tough and I crashed the aircraft many times.

I realized I was heading in the direction of Tampa, Florida, and this was clearly my mission. I had followed I-95 south for some time when I saw the cluster of buildings on the distant horizon. I somehow knew it was my destination. Using a dead-reckoning type of navigation, I turned southwest somewhere north of Orlando. I had never been to Tampa except passing through on I-275 or I-4.

I estimated I was fifty miles or so from my destination when, to my great astonishment, I saw four massive tornados come into view behind Tampa. These tornadoes were coming straight at me, and they were all category 5's. I could see the debris they were sucking up from the ground.

Until this point, I had been actually enjoying myself; but this was when I realized I was dreaming. However, it had validity in my real-life experiences and in what I call my "book of dreams".

Have you ever been in a dream so realistic that it was a disappointment when you realized it wasn't real? Dreams with color and great detail were somewhat common to me, but I'll admit this dream was by far the best, when considering the circumstances and my sensory-emotional state.

The colors were so vivid and bright, and I could see across the entire peninsula of the state of Florida. I even remember smelling subtropical aromas. This dream was high definition for sure.

Once I realized I was dreaming, it made sense why I was having so much fun flying this helicopter, and why I wasn't stressed that I might crash and die. The four tornadoes I was approaching had me concerned, though, and I found myself contemplating my next course of action.

While in my dream, I recalled asking the Lord a question sometime before while I was awake. I had prayed and asked Jesus, "If I am in the last moments just before I die, will I call out Your name for help? Or will I cuss at the situation, showing my true heart?"

I was raised to love Jesus and worship Him. Nevertheless, life throws curveballs at you along the way which can force you off the path to spending eternity with the One True God.

Still flying, I wordlessly made a decision regarding the tornadoes. I planned to fly the agile helicopter westerly toward New Port Richey, then turn south and follow the coast to the opening of Tampa Bay. Finally, making a hard-left and flying over the Skyway Bridge, I'd come into Tampa behind the tornadoes. I thought to myself, *I am so clever.* Immediately, an audible voice, stern yet calm, said, "Julian, you must pick one of the tornadoes and fly the helicopter through it and land in Tampa."

My concern instantly escalated. I was scared. I questioned why I couldn't pursue my plan of skirting around the tornadoes. This time the voice telepathically reiterated that my plan was forbidden.

Somehow, I knew there would be enormous consequences if I disobeyed. I protested again, saying the little helicopter would never withstand these massive tornadoes and I would surely die. The voice said, "If you find yourself fearful, call on My name." Even in my dream I knew it was Jesus speaking to me.

While dreaming, there are things you know without further evidence, and I knew it was Jesus speaking to me. I contemplated the four F-5 tornadoes before me and thought, *these storms are something I have to go through.*

I had three children and my wife, so I started feeling the storms must represent them. From left to right, I named the storms after my wife, Stephanie, then my oldest daughter, my middle daughter, and my youngest son on the far right. The left storm, which I named after my wife, was far left of Tampa. That storm looked fierce, with dark clouds and much debris; I knew better than to go through that storm. I also thought, *we have been through so much already, I don't want to go through another storm with her.*

I chose the second tornado from the far right. I knew my middle child had fought through several dark, hard situations, and I thought perhaps me going through her storm would help her in some way.

As I continually approached Tampa, the tornadoes grew to be giants. The dream was so real, with debris smacking against the helicopter and the little chopper was being tossed left and right... and I was still about ten miles from entering the tornado. Both hands on the stick, I tried to keep the helicopter steady.

I did not readily accept the situation before me. I was under great duress.

Have you ever been in a situation where you knew you had to go through something very tough- ultimately testing you— but you knew you would come out on the other end a much better person? So, you face it instead of cowering and running from it? This was one of those things I knew I had to go through. There was no backing out, even though I knew I was going to crash and burn.

It was as if the giant vortex of the tornado was now slowly pulling me toward it. I was trying to control the direction and rate of speed, but the helicopter was more out of control than ever before. The wind was whistling fiercely through small, unseen pinholes in the cockpit. Somehow dust was getting in, and the cockpit started to fill with it. I was increasingly losing control of the helicopter. It wouldn't be long before I'd get sucked into this huge, ferocious giant of water, debris, and turbulent air.

Before I knew it, I was inside the vicious giant of a demon.

The helicopter went sideways, much like the times I was flying on the simulator, but knee jerk pulls on the stick made no difference. Then, violently, the helicopter turned upside down and started to roll and spin. The G forces were too much for me, and I began to lose consciousness. I sensed my eyes beginning to move back into my head.

I called out to Jesus for help.

In my almost unconscious state of mind, I was yelling, "Jesus, I need you! Jesus, help!" I was fearful. I knew, without a doubt, I was going to die a horrible death in this tornado. Still in my dream, I believe I became unconscious because it wasn't long before the helicopter stopped shaking violently.

I was through the storm. Debris was still hitting the exterior of the aircraft, but the dust started to dissipate in the cockpit, and I began to level off. My arms to my side, I was feeling fragile as I came out of unconsciousness.

The helicopter was flying by itself, still moving forward— over and through the tall buildings of Tampa. I could see a helicopter landing pad just ahead near the water. My altitude was now between two or three hundred feet. I remember being worried that the blades would clip one of the buildings, or even a tall palm tree, as I descended. Again, knowing things that one does while dreaming— like unwritten rules— I was forbidden to touch the controls because I would only make things worse. To be honest, I didn't want to fly anymore, not after what I had just been through. I was done. I wanted to be on the ground.

As the helicopter maneuvered in and above the pad, I was once again apprehensive about the palm trees and the buildings.

My worries were unwarranted. Jesus said, "Your landing in Tampa is going to be perfect," and it was. The helicopter came to rest perfectly and precisely on the helipad, right next to large buildings and the Hillsborough River.

As the blades slowed and the door of the little helicopter opened, I instinctively knew the building I was at was a courthouse.

I slowly walked up to it, and was reaching to pull open the large glass doors, when the dream ended.

Carried Away from the Marital Castle

"See to it that no one takes you captive through hollow and deceptive philosophy..." Colossians 2:8

It was the summer of 2015, and I was on my way to Boy Scout camp with my son and other boy scouts. It was going to be a hot day, with temperatures in the upper 90's. Riding shotgun in the van, my mind wandered to my dissatisfaction with life. Something was missing, even though I had everything. My wife, Stephanie, was wholly committed to me, and I had beautiful, grown, healthy children.

I loved Stephanie more than anything. She was the bride of my youth, and she made me feel grounded and true about myself. She was by far the biggest blessing I had ever received in my life; I knew I didn't deserve her. In spite of that, I was getting ready to do something to her in the next year that was downright ugly and mean. Clouded by stress, finances, shame, guilt, and memories of my failures, I lost sight of my love for her.

One of my hobbies at the time was a HO scale model railroad train village that I'd been working on in the basement since 2005. I would also sail a little 17-foot sailboat on nearby lakes when all the correct criteria lined up (such as good wind, free weekends, and a sailing partner). Matching those three up would prove challenging, sometimes all I could line up was good wind and a free weekend.

During that time, my blood pressure was spiking, and I felt awful on the medicine prescribed me. The doctor gave me an ultimatum, "If you want to stay alive, either exercise and lose weight, or continue to take the meds."

Still in the van traveling to camp, I was brought back to reality when one of the scouts escalated noises, making a ruckus in the back of the van. I was the Scoutmaster of a Boy Scout Troop, and I had 98 scouts in the troop at the time (13 of whom were in the van), including my son.

We camped at least once a month, sometimes up to three times a month. We hiked parts of the Appalachian Trail in Virginia, Tennessee, and North Carolina. We camped at Crazy Horse in South Dakota, and we crossed the Colorado River at 3 AM at the bottom of the Grand Canyon. Just about every weekend, we were doing an activity such as kayaking, canoeing, white-water rafting, climbing, backpacking, "hammocking," and swimming.

All the crazy action drew the boys in; they were coming from everywhere to join the troop. On the flip side, all the time away from my wife didn't help our relationship whatsoever— it was pushing us apart.

We arrived at the camp, where I focused on spending time with my son and the other boys.

During that time, Stephanie was staying focused on our family, managing relationships with our children, family, and friends from church. She frequently made herself part of small groups and Bible studies, and she handled all the crises our family experienced.

When I wasn't camping with the Boy Scouts, my wife and I attended church separately. Our son loved serving at the church. That meant he had to be there Saturday evening, early Sunday morning, and stay until after 1 PM. I wanted to save gas and mileage on our cars, so I took him to church on Sunday morning and stayed for the first service. As I left, Stephanie and I would pass each other on her way to the second service— after which she would bring our son home.

We thought it incredible that he loved to be at church, and that he had such a heart for serving in various capacities, so we wanted to encourage it. Looking back, there had to be a better way. Perhaps I could have served the first service and attended the second with my precious wife, but I was still wandering in the desert. My heart wasn't ready for that kind of commitment.

When 2016 rolled around, I was walking five miles a day, increasing my metabolism and getting my body fit. My wife wasn't interested in walking with me, so I had friends come along instead.

Stephanie and I were drifting apart. I was fighting off attractions with other women, and telling myself I couldn't go down that road.

The Boy Scout troop was heading to the Grand Canyon in the summer of 2016, and I wanted to be in the best shape possible. At the same time, I was feeling my life had little purpose, and I wasn't valued at home. I kept telling myself the highlight of my life was not supposed to be walking to the mailbox every day, or mowing five acres of grass each week. I was not going to do that for the rest of my life.

I dreamed of owning a forty-foot sailboat and sailing again. In the military, I had been stationed remotely for a year on a small island about 800 miles southwest of Hawaii. Unfortunately, the twelve-month tour was branded as "unaccompanied" by the military, so Stephanie had to stay in Kentucky.

To get my mind off of being away from my wife and family, I had taken advantage of every free moment to become scuba certified. I also taught myself to sail on the boats provided by the recreational department of the military, and I loved it!

After those twelve months were up, Stephanie was finally able to join me on Oahu, Hawaii, for three years. We both loved Hawaii. I had become a member of two yacht clubs. I would sail in and around the islands of Hawaii with friends, and my love of sailing continued to grow.

Now I would spend hours on the internet looking at sailboats for sale on the east coast and Florida. I knew my wife would never go for it; she was fearful of water after a near-drowning experience as a child. We talked about getting a place in Florida and spending a lot of time between there and our home in Kentucky. She dreamed of living near Disney World. I dreamed of Florida's west coast.

Over the years, we had developed some Godly habits to keep ourselves from being devoured by the evil one. One such habit was getting up early in the morning to pray and read the Bible. I believe we were trying hard to follow the wisdom in 1 Peter 5:8:

"Be sober [well balanced and self-disciplined], be alert and cautious at all times. That the enemy of yours, the devil prowls around like a roaring lion [fiercely hungry], seeking someone to devour." 1 Peter 5:8 (AMP)

"But I am afraid that just as Eve was deceived by the serpent's cunning, your minds may somehow be led astray from your sincere and pure devotion to Christ." 2 Corinthians 11:3

I thought I was above being deceived. I went to church, read my Bible, and convinced myself that being deceived wouldn't happen to me. All along, God was trying to alert me; if I would have opened my spiritual eyes, I would've seen His warnings. Stephanie saw them and tried to caution me, but I would not listen.

I loved God, and I knew He loved me. I knew I had to stay plugged into church to keep myself from falling away. Time and time again, my relationship with Him would be so good; then, almost as if turning off a switch, I would be heading in the wrong direction. I felt like I was a mature Christian who could recognize attacks from the Devil, but I was deceived. I did not foresee the attack that was coming—an attack on my marriage and soul. The evil one was slowly seducing me, and I had no idea it was happening. My conscience was subdued, and at some point, it became silent.

Soon Stephanie and I were sleeping in separate rooms. My excuse was her snoring, but in truth I probably kept her up with *my* snoring. We were falling apart, arguing about little things, and not enjoying each other's company. I couldn't remember the last time we went out on a date. I felt as if our relationship was heading nowhere. I saw myself as a failure. When I felt discouraged, or when I wasn't succeeding at my standards, is when I became most vulnerable. Satan had me right where he wanted me. I tried so hard to hold it together, but my morals were unraveling.

The idea of sailing in Florida consumed me and became an idol that I dreamed about daily. I would sometimes escape the monotony of daily life through daydreaming of being on a sailboat. I even thought about it at bedtime to help me fall asleep. I'd had fantasies about women before, but never about a way of life like this.

The idea of having my own sailing yacht is what I worshiped, but that wasn't the only affair I had. I managed to turn the smiles and attention of another woman into emotions that later became physical. Again, Stephanie tried to warn me. She saw, and knew in her heart, what was happening. She confronted me numerous times, but I always denied any wrongdoing. This caused even further distance between us. I didn't want to admit the sin I was involved in, and she desperately wanted to protect not only her heart, but also the hearts of our children.

I was feeling good physically, but emotionally I was a train wreck waiting to happen. Stressed from working day in and day out, I had a lot of pressure on my shoulders with finances. I pictured myself in quicksand and trying to get out— the more I struggled against it, the deeper I slipped in.

I felt as if all this weight was on my shoulders alone. I felt disrespected at home and started believing my family only wanted one thing from me— to keep food on the table and a roof over their heads. This perception led to being disgruntled and feeling even more disrespected.

Truth be told, my actions were causing distrust between me and Stephanie. Satan was lying to me in the spiritual realm (later, the Holy Spirit showed me in a vision that I was bound and gagged by the enemy, in preparation to be carried away from our marital castle).

The trips away with the Boy Scouts were my escape, and I genuinely enjoyed being with my son. It wasn't a vacation by any means, but at least it was an escape. I often cried out to God to rescue me from the pressure I was in, but I felt nothing in response. That was hard for me, because so often in the past when I'd cried out to God He had responded in mysterious ways. I felt like the Israelites must have felt, wandering in the desert in search of the promised land. This time He wasn't there— or so it felt. I didn't realize it at the time, but God was using those circumstances to build my character, even though I was choosing the wrong path yet again.

In early June, I returned from a week at the Grand Canyon with over 128 scouts and family members. I was feeling terrific about myself physically, and a little better emotionally. The time hiking and camping in the canyon was refreshing. I was confident, and everything looked different to me. My view and opinion of the rest of my life changed; the image of me walking out to the mailbox and mowing 5 acres of grass every week for the rest of my life was fading. I started to say no to that life. My thought process was that, if I played my cards just right, I could be reeling in the sunshine and breathing in the fresh ocean air while sailing on Florida's west coast by 2017.

Father's Day in 2016 was a disappointment for me. It was a beautiful, sunny, windy day. I wanted to take a picnic lunch to one of the local lakes and get out on the water with my family. I had taken my kids sailing once while on vacation in Clearwater, Florida, and they had loved it. My son had been sailing with me on other occasions as well.

On Father's Day, my oldest daughter and her husband were sick, my other two children weren't interested, and Stephanie didn't want to get out in a boat on the water due to her previous near-drowning experience. So, I went by myself.

It was a great day to sail! Winds were excellent, and the lake was almost empty. From a distance, I saw a family start to assemble their sailboat. As we sailed past each other, I checked it off in my mind: father, mother, and children, all spending the day together on Father's Day. Just another incident that helped convince me that I was unhappy.

July was approaching, and I knew I would be away from home again with scouting events. The first was a week-long hike on the Appalachian Trail. That week apart distanced Stephanie and me even more, since the lack of cell service contributed to almost no communication between us for the entire week.

Earlier in the year, Stephanie and I had planned a trip to Florida for August. That trip was to have a two-fold purpose: one was to celebrate 31 years of marriage together; the second was to explore central Florida and the west coast, near St. Petersburg. It was a two-week trip to look at houses, and I had even contacted boat brokers to scope out a few sailboats. My fingers were crossed, and I was hoping that somehow Stephanie would see things my way.

We planned to get a house in central Florida, somewhere north or west of Disney World, since one of Stephanie's dreams was to work there. She loves Disney!

Her love for Disney began at the age of six, when her Grandparents took her to the Magic Kingdom in its opening year; and it was reinforced year after year as she visited her Grandparents, who lived in Debary, Florida. Once she became an adult, she was hooked, and shared her affection of Disney with our children. The sailboat on Florida's Suncoast was my Disney, and I wanted to share that with my children as well.

We were having fun looking at houses, and dreaming about how moving to Florida would work out, all while I was trying to hide the affair I was having with another woman. To make this Florida dream happen, selling our home in Kentucky was our ticket.

One evening, Stephanie and I were out for dinner, and I opened the sunroof in the rental car to enjoy the ocean breeze. We were in a discussion about our moving plans, and I commented on us having a house in central Florida. I said, "When I get the sailboat, I'll dock it on the west coast and spend the weekend sailing. Since you'll probably be working at Disney through the weekend, I'm not going to sit in hot central Florida with a sailboat waiting for me." I continued, "When the weather is bad, I'll stay home."

Stephanie immediately replied, "What did you say?" I repeated myself, and she became angry. An argument ensued. Stephanie blurted out, "If spending the weekends on a sailboat is your intention, then we might as well get a divorce."

Perfect! I thought, *there is my permission, and her agreement, to get a divorce*. I threw that in her face for the next year to come. I'm not even sure if we went out to eat that night, we were both so angry about our differences with the Florida plan— and neither of us wanted to give in.

I felt that 70-80% of the decision was mine to make, since I worked and brought in the money. Not to mention, I would be the one paying for the house and the sailboat, anyway. However, she had good reasons for her doubt and anger. I couldn't be trusted on the west coast of Florida on a forty-foot sailboat, let alone anywhere else.

For the last week of our vacation, she went to the beach to watch sunsets by herself, spending hours alone. I walked in the early mornings and visited the heated pool by myself. We slept in separate rooms. It was one of the most miserable Florida vacations ever.

Many aspects of my 2015, "Flying to Florida" dream was unfolding right before my eyes. I started to believe that dream was my destiny.

After returning from the Florida trip, things were even worse between me and Stephanie. I was upset that Stephanie was willing to work for Disney but not ready to get a job back home to help out with the finances. The perfect storm was in motion, and I was getting sucked in by my actions and attitudes.

Although the word divorce came up on our Florida trip, it was only briefly discussed. I could tell it surprised her that we were now considering it to this level. I started to realize the storm in my dream was not something my middle daughter and I would go through, but perhaps the storm was a divorce me and Stephanie would go through.

Once back at home, I made more comments about getting a divorce, and we briefly discussed splitting our possessions. I secretly opened a new checking account and told Stephanie I wanted to take over the finances.

I decided, while on the Appalachian trail hiking trip, that if she didn't like my idea of us having a house in central

Florida and me spending weekends on the sailboat, then it was her loss. I wasn't giving in on this; I'd made up my mind.

Even in our daily lives, our decision making was rarely balanced. Our roles as parents had become distorted due to us being in the military for over twenty years. I was often deployed, at which times she was father, mother, principal, teacher, "enforcer" – everything. All the various roles that are usually shared between parents, she performed by herself. Because of that, she had an amazing relationship with each of our children.

Although I had been retired since 2005, nothing had changed with the decision-making in our family. She always had the last word, and the decision would always go her way. I was tired of never having a say about our life, our children, or our marriage.

As time went on, Stephanie and I had increasingly detailed conversations about how to divide our things. I was surprised she was discussing things so openly and not pushing back. I got the feeling she was playing along, thinking I would soon give in and put all the divorce talk to bed. In retrospect, I now know she was just tired; she was tired of my continued pattern of infidelity, and saw this as possibly the only way those patterns would ever stop. She had no fight left in her.

In September, while on a business trip to Pennsylvania and Virginia, I thought a great deal about everything. Our future looked messy, and I didn't want to spend the rest of my life unhappy. The business trip was supposed to be one week long. However, I started thinking about extending my trip to make it look like I was still traveling for an extra week. Instead of going back home, I decided to fly to Clearwater, Florida, to look for a place to live. I picked Clearwater because of the beautiful beaches, the inter-coastal waterways, and I knew of a sailing club there that I was convinced would bring me happiness.

I knew I was in uncharted waters. I had never before flown to another state under the ruse that I was somewhere else. Before this, I always would have let Stephanie know where I was when traveling on business. More and more, I was drawn to the "Flying to Florida" dream, thinking that Tampa was just a metaphor of a place I would go in Florida. In my mind, if I landed anywhere on the west coast, I would be happy.

While in Clearwater, I searched for a place to live. I planned to secure an apartment, go home, pack my belongings, and drive back to Florida. One evening, at a beach bar listening to the waves roll in, the woman next to me struck up a conversation. She learned I was looking for a place to live in Clearwater, and that I wasn't having much luck finding the ideal place. She then told me her boyfriend was looking for a housemate in Tampa. It was as if she was a salesperson; she was setting me up and trying to close on the deal. I agreed to take a look at it the next day, because I was flying back to Kentucky in just a few days.

Once in Tampa, my eyes started to sparkle as we entered a gated community near the water. Inside the gate, there was a red brick road, and the landscaping was immaculate. I was thinking, *this can't be true. God is taking care of me! He **does** want me to be happy.*

I arrived at the house and rang the doorbell. A very polite man, named Jack, answered the door and welcomed me in. He was about 5'8", in his mid-fifties, and in good physical shape. He was a divorced insurance salesman with three adult children.

The condo had a two-car garage and office on the first floor. The second floor was a kitchen, dining room, living room, and balcony. On the third floor, there was a master bedroom and bath that belonged to Jack, and two other bedrooms that shared a standard full bath.

The condo was beautiful; fully furnished, with white carpet throughout. It had all-new conveniences, such as Corian countertops, modern light fixtures, and lastly, an elevator. Yes, an elevator!

Jack took me on a short tour of the community and clubhouse. The private clubhouse was fabulous, with its own restaurant, two heated swimming pools, and a tiki-bar on the pool deck. While poolside, Tampa Bay was just a few feet away. The tropically-landscaped pool decks were emphasized with some lovely women soaking up the sun. Jack shared that several professional sport stars lived a few houses down the street.

I couldn't believe my eyes, this was happening just like my "Flying to Florida" dream! I was now convinced the storm in my dream was the divorce, and that, just like in my dream, everything would turn out okay.

Back at the condo, I gave Jack my first months' rent. I shared my story about filing for a divorce, and I planned that I would be back around the beginning of November.

After returning home, I couldn't stop thinking about leaving Kentucky and getting to my new place. I began to plan my departure.

Our children knew things were bad between me and Stephanie, but they were not prepared for the storm that was barreling toward them. One day we sat them down and let them know we were discussing divorce. I don't recall their exact reactions, probably because I was so self-centered it wouldn't have mattered if they had strong opinions or not. Thinking back, I was worried about how my son would take the news. He seemed to be okay at the time, but I now know that it was just a facade. He was hurt.

In spite of our conversation, no one had any idea that I was getting ready to leave them and move to Florida.

During my lunch break on October 23rd, 2016, I drove to the lawyer's office and filed for divorce. I didn't tell Stephanie what I had done. On the drive home, I had a sickening feeling of failure. I thought, *what have I done?* I think I felt ill because of the verse in Malachi regarding divorce:

"The man who hates and divorces his wife," says the LORD, *the God of Israel, "does violence to the one he*

should protect," says the LORD *Almighty. So be on your guard, and do not be unfaithful. Malachi 2:16*

I didn't realize how much God hates it when covenants (promises) are broken. I had crossed the line. Stephanie and God would not be happy with me, but I justified myself by thinking *this isn't the contract I signed up for. I'm not going to put up with being disrespected, being in an unhappy marriage, and carrying all the financial stress and burden.* I conveniently forgot my wedding vows "for better or for worse, for richer or poorer."

I was influenced by a society which has diminished the meaning of covenants (promises) down to self-centered nothingness.

I worried about my children, even though my youngest was just a few years away from being an adult. What would they think? How would they react?

I could hear the pacifying voices of friends, work associates, and others, all reassuring me that, "Kids are tough. They'll bounce back. It will take time, but they'll be ok." I added to this false assurance by thinking, *my children love their mother much more than they love me — Father's Day proved that. They'll be fine, they won't even realize I'm gone.*

Even though I didn't believe those voices, I went with it. I was in a dark fog. I knew the right answers, but they weren't adding up with reality. Half the time, I knew what God said in His Word regarding divorce; the other half of the time, I was being convinced through a sort of spiritual "brain fog" to pursue a divorce. This "brain fog" was my free will.

My parents would be disappointed, too. I justified that thought with, *this is my life, not my parents'.*

When I returned home, Stephanie asked where I had been. I didn't tell her I had filed for divorce.

Common sense told me that I needed to take care of them, financially. I loved my kids. I told myself that I would always love Stephanie, but that didn't mean I had to spend the rest of my life with her. Although I feel there were other significant spiritual forces at play in my actions, I ultimately made the decisions and executed those actions. I have confessed before God, and I take full responsibility for what I did.

Looking back, I didn't heed the warnings contained in Scripture, such as:

So then, just as you received Christ Jesus as Lord, continue to live your lives in him, rooted and built up in him, strengthened in faith as you were taught, and overflowing with thankfulness. <u>See to it that no one takes you captive through hollow and deceptive philosophy</u>, which depends on *human tradition and the elemental spiritual forces rather than on Christ. Colossians 2:6-8 (emphasis added)*

    Then it happened; one day, near the end of October, my wife and children (including my son-in-law and grandson) went to the zoo. I immediately started packing up just the stuff I could fit in my car. Once I had packed up, I left. I didn't leave a note or anything. Later that night, Stephanie texted me and asked where I was; I had built up so much anger toward her that I don't recall if I even replied that evening.

    Eventually, perhaps a few days later, I told her that I had moved out and wouldn't be back. I told her that I would contact our children and let them know. Although I genuinely did not want to hurt her, I was angry; I felt the world was coming down around me. I cowardly walked out the door and never looked back. I moved to Florida and left my wife and family behind without even telling them.

Chapter 2

Leaving the 99

My landing in Tampa was completely laced with selfishness. I lived in an awesome yacht club community, minutes from the waters of Tampa Bay. I didn't have to mow the grass anymore. I didn't even have to walk to the mailbox, because the mail was brought to me. I had few responsibilities. I walked and swam daily in heated swimming pools. I went to the beach often and soaked up the Florida rays.

The story of the lost sheep is recorded in both *Mathew 18:12* and *Luke 15:4*. We are told that the Shepherd (Jesus) will leave His sheep grazing in the pasture to start searching for the one that went astray.

Jesus will leave the 99 sheep to find His 1 lost sheep.

As time went on, He started calling me by name. He spoke to me through others; through messages at church, and real-life examples of people's situations.

It was incredibly important to me that I keep up my relationship with God — or at least the version that allowed me to stay on my present course. I visited several churches, trying to find a place to worship. At the same time, I immersed myself in local social groups to help me forget about my real life. I was delusional, using my "Flying to Florida" dream as justification that the transition to Florida was God's way of providing for me to be happy.

In hindsight, I had two conflicting relationships going at the same time: my relationship with God, and my relationship with the world.

My relationship with God was one-way. I was communicating with Him and attending church, but I was not listening to what He wanted for my life — only what I fooled myself into *thinking* He wanted. I had just walked out on my family, and the covenant vows I had made before God to my wife.

I was toying with the world in the social groups I joined while in Florida. Until I truly repented of my sin, and corrected my ways by patching things up with my family, I knew God's hands were tied in assisting me with reconciliation.

I'm sure He wasn't amused at all. It was like I was calling, but nobody was on the other end. Until I made the declaration that I had made mistakes— that I had sinned against Him, my wife, my family— there would be no answer. He was trying to get my attention all along, I just wasn't listening.

My relationship with the world took shape in my social groups. I had one foot in the world, and one foot barely in the church. I was trying to satisfy my desire to have fun in the world, be politically correct, and in line with God's word at the same time. The problem was that God's Word says we can't do both (1 John 2:15). I was trying to make the impossible work.

My social groups should have been with like-minded believers in Christ, not people with beliefs that spanned from Buddhism to the universe itself being god. The Scriptures are clear about "other gods."

"For great is the LORD and most worthy of praise; He is to be feared above all gods." Psalm 96:4

"For you, LORD, are the Most High over all the earth; you are exalted far above all gods." Psalm 97:9

"And God spoke all these words: 'I am the Lord your God, who brought you out of Egypt, out of the land of slavery. You shall have no other gods before Me.'" Exodus 20:1-3

When I would meet people in social groups, I made it clear that I had a strong faith in God, even if my current actions didn't reflect that. Usually, someone would say "Yeah, well, I believe the Universe is god, and we all came about by evolution." My spirit would cringe, and I would move in a new direction to continue the search for someone who could help me feel fulfilled. It was so delusional to believe that I could fulfill my worldly desires and have a true relationship with Jesus at the same time.

Just over a month after moving to Florida, I made the 15-hour drive back to Kentucky for the holidays. It turned out to be the worst Christmas I'd ever experienced. Stephanie and I were not communicating at all, and to make matters worse, she was recovering from a surgery she'd had earlier in the month— at a time when I was nowhere to assist her.

I wanted a relationship with my children, and by going back to Kentucky I was stepping back into the world of reality. Although my children were completely angry with me (two-out-of-three denied me any time with them on Christmas Day), they all gave me about 3-4 hours the day after Christmas. They were keeping their distance, even though we were in the same room. I could see and feel their anger and hurting hearts in their actions and words. There were moments in those few hours that felt like everything was moving in slow motion.

Seeing my children like this should have been enough to turn me around. I would tell myself, *you're such a loser*. I could see my children hurting, and I knew in my heart that broken homes damaged children, regardless of their age. I knew studies proved that children need a father and a mother; it's the way God intended.

I *wanted* to believe the voices from friends, coworkers, and some family that said, "They'll be fine, it will take time, but they will come out ok on the other side of divorce. It'll just take time." I wanted to drown out the reality of what I saw in my children.

Sadly, Christmas was over. Feeling dejected and disappointed in myself for the decision I had made, I decided to leave a day early for my return trip to Florida. I planned to drive all night, straight through. During that drive, I had to pull over to the side of the road because I couldn't see through my tears. I was hurting. I cried out to God to help me, to give me peace. I asked Him if He was listening.

Nothing. I got nothing back. He wasn't listening— or so it seemed.

In reality, He *was* listening, but He was waiting on me to take the step of repentance. Even though I felt that pursuing a life in Florida was something I had to do to be happy, I was no longer entirely sure about my actions. I was second-guessing myself because of the pain I was causing my wife and children. I put hours and hours of thought into the steps I had taken, and what my future would look like.

"What do you think? If a man owns a hundred sheep, and one of them wanders away, will he not leave the ninety-nine on the hills and go to look for the one that wandered off?" Matthew 18:12

God's Pursuit of the Captive

Back in Florida, I submerged myself into local social groups. I was meeting new people 2-3 times a week, meanwhile trying to put distance between my wife and me. I was separating myself from my family.

I hadn't had many guy friends in Kentucky, so it was one of my goals while in Florida to build some "bro" relationships. I met several guys and women who, just like me, had left their wives, husbands, and children in pursuit of their version of happiness. People would ask me, "What brought you to Florida"? I would say, "My marriage didn't work out, so I moved to Florida to sail." Everyone seemed to think that was a good move on my part. Many would say, "good for you!"

One evening, while hanging out in one of the social groups, I met a successful pilot of a major airline named Derik. He confessed that he came to Florida to sail as well, having made the transition about ten years before. He was divorced and had three boys. Derik invited me to sail the following weekend on his 45-foot sailboat.

I showed up early to his house that Saturday. He lived on one of the canals to the Gulf coast. There, in his back yard, was his 45-foot sailboat. He could simply walk out of his back door, take a few steps, and be standing on his sailboat. It had three cabins, three heads, the mainsail, and a jib.

I thought, *wow! What are the odds I would befriend a guy with a sailboat similar to what I wanted?* Derik informed me that more friends were on the way to come sailing with us. We talked for a bit while he drank coffee and I drank a bottle of water. Pictures of his now-grown boys were on his lamp tables and walls. I started asking questions about what led up to his divorce and how it became settled. He shared how it all happened.

When he started sharing his story, I felt ashamed; I thought *how selfish I was, to leave my family, to abandon my wife and children, son-in-law, and newborn grandson, all so I could sail and have no responsibilities.* You see, Derik had done the same thing I did. One day, without notice, he left his family and moved to Florida. I thought, *how selfish of him to leave three teenage boys and his wife.* It was the pot calling the kettle black. I had done the same thing to my family, how selfish of me.

I finished the day on the water with Derik and friends, and I had a lot to think about on the drive back to Tampa.

I couldn't get over the fact that I had found a friend in someone who left their family just as I had done. I thought for sure I was alone — there couldn't be anyone as bad as me.

The drive back to Tampa from the coast was about an hour, and my mind was racing the entire time. Was God showing me something here? I knew, from the many times I'd read the Bible, that there were examples of spiritual activity happening on our behalf. Just behind this life of reality is a veil of angels working for our good; and likewise, evil spirits are working to destroy us.

An excellent example of the spiritual veil is found in 2 Kings 6:8-23:

"When the servant of the man of God got up and went out early the next morning, an army with horses and chariots had surrounded the city. 'Oh no, my lord! What shall we do?' the servant asked. 'Don't be afraid,' the prophet answered. 'Those who are with us are more than those who are with them.' And Elisha prayed, 'Open his eyes, LORD, so that he may see.' Then the LORD opened the servant's eyes, and he looked and saw the hills full of horses and chariots of fire all around Elisha. As the enemy came down toward him, Elisha prayed to the LORD, 'Strike this army with blindness.' So, he struck them with blindness, as Elisha had asked." 2 Kings 6:15-18

In this example, the prophet, Elisha, and his servant found themselves surrounded by the large Aram army which was sent to destroy "the man of God." The young servant was in terrible fear for his life and cried out to Elisha, who told him, "Don't be afraid; there are more on our side than on theirs." (2 Kings 6:16) He then asked God to open the young man's eyes so he could see. The Lord opened the young man's eyes, and he saw that the hillside around Elisha was filled with horses and chariots of fire. The army he saw was of a spiritual nature — and they had the Aramean army surrounded. The story goes on; the Aramean army was blinded and spared the wrath of the heavenly horses and chariots of fire. The young man and Elisha went unscathed from the incident.

Just like in the story of Elisha, Angels are assigned for our good, and evil spirits are trying to destroy us.

"For our struggle is not against flesh and blood, but against the rulers, against the authorities, against the powers of this dark world and against the spiritual forces of evil in the heavenly realms." Ephesians 6:12

In the spiritual world, the Holy Spirit was searching for me in all the dark places, like one of his lost sheep. He wouldn't physically step across "free will" and take me, but He sure would call my name and let me know He was looking for me. He was showing me the truth through examples like Derik; his example helped me see the reality of my own actions.

You may ask, "Who exactly is this Holy Spirit?" Jesus describes the Holy Spirit in John 15:26 and 16:7.

"When the Advocate comes, whom I will send to you from the Father—the Spirit of truth who goes out from the Father—he will testify about me." John 15:26

"But very truly I tell you, it is for your good that I am going away. Unless I go away, the Advocate will not come to you; but if I go, I will send him to you." John 16:7

He tells us the "advocate" comes from the Father. He's the Spirit of Truth, who testifies about Jesus. I love the Jewish name for the Holy Spirit: *Ruach Ha-Kodesh* [רוח הקודש] which, plainly translated, means "the Spirit of YHWH" (God).

I was later shown through a vision that our marriage was much like a castle, designed to protect the whole family. However, our fortress had been breached through a crack in my personal foundations.

The foundational cracks were caused by sin.

Many of the attacks throughout my life that caused damage to me and my family were, indeed, caused by my sin. Jesus is the spiritual leader of the church. Through this example I believe it is the man's role to be priests of their home because the head of every man is Christ.

"But I want you to realize that the head of every man is Christ, and the head of the woman is man, and the head of Christ is God." 1 Corinthians 11:3

"And He put all things under His feet, and gave Him to be head over all things to the church." Ephesians 1:22

I found that there were many men and women in Florida with a story similar to mine. They all had their justification for divorce based in reality, but in the spiritual realm it was obvious that one, or both, parties had become deceived by the one who is determined to kill, steal, and destroy (John 10:10). They hadn't all left their families like I had, but they all gave up; they quit trying to make it work, and the vows they recited on their wedding day no longer meant anything to them. I knew God wasn't happy about the situation in Florida, where so many were abandoning their spouses and families to live the "salt life".

The salt lifestyle is ocean-centric, with activities like powerboating, surfing, windsurfing, kite-boarding, scuba diving, sailing, and fishing— to name a few. It was the life I wanted too. I wanted to be active on the water, to feel the wind in my face and in my sails, with the warm sun on my skin. Although I knew God wasn't happy with men and women trading in their families for this lifestyle, it wasn't enough to turn me around. In my right ear I had a voice telling me "this is happening so you can be happy."

I went to church regularly, and even joined a men's small group. I drove 45-60 minutes one-way to the small group every week to meet with like-minded believers. It was my attempt to stay connected to the Lord.

In the small group, we talked about how to be men of honor. Kind of ironic, right? It was the Holy Spirit's way of gently reminding me of what He expected from me. Every sermon I listened to resonated, as if it was drafted with me in mind. I often found myself in tears, especially during praise and worship songs.

I tried to understand it, and I thought about it a lot. I genuinely asked myself why tears would start flowing during praise and worship songs at church, or even in my car. Was I sad? Was this my body's way of showing all the emotions I had pent up?

After much thought, I believed the tears were because my soul was crying out. I was condemned for my sins— my spirit knew I was wrong, but my flesh didn't want to change.

When at church, I wanted to worship God, but there was a conflict; I would raise my hands to worship Him, but in reality, I was just trying to convince my spirit that my relationship with Jesus was "ok." I wasn't raising my hands during worship because I wanted to worship Him, I did it because I needed to feel Jesus was there. However, He wouldn't acknowledge me until I fully repented of my actions, and I wasn't ready to do that yet. I had more I wanted to discover in Florida.

Back in Kentucky, Stephanie's friends, neighbors, and even some family members, told her to leave me and never look back. I don't blame them for telling her that, I was a train on its way to destruction. She submerged herself into a small group of strong, Godly women from church. They listened to her, prayed with her, and asked, "What is God telling you?"

"The LORD is longsuffering and abundant in mercy, forgiving iniquity and transgression; but He by no means clears the guilty, visiting the iniquity of the fathers on the children to the third and fourth generation." Numbers 14:18 (NKJV)

Divorce Court: Take One

In February of 2017, I flew back to Kentucky for our first court date. While waiting for our case to be heard, I listened in on another divorce case as it was unfolding. Divorce court was new to me, so I listened intently. It was a man in his mid-thirties, being torn away from his wife and children. His wife was the petitioner. She filed for divorce and was requesting full custody of their two small boys. The wife was young and beautiful, dressed professionally. I wondered what had happened, and I drew assumptions on the matter. Could it be she went to work after the boys were born and met someone who appealed to her feelings?

The man, unlike me, was an emotional mess. You could tell he was a good father to his boys based on his comments about them. He still loved her, too— he mentioned it several times.

The judge told the couple that the boys would live with the mother, and they would share custody fifty-fifty. The man turned to the judge, and then his wife, saying, "I don't want this! Please, we don't have to do this, I forgive you. We can work it out." It was as if he was pleading with the judge, but at the same time his soon-to-be divorced wife. The man broke down and started to weep as he asked, "Why? Why? Why?"

"I don't want this, please," he spoke to the judge, and he begged his wife. Her jaw clenched, she showed silent indifference. Something in me said, "She is just as deceived as I am."

In our day-to-day life, we tend to take our spouse for granted. We stop showing them how much we love them, we stop communicating with them, and we stop treating them the way we did when we first met them. Then our eye and mind wanders to someone outside of our marriage who appeals to us.

What is happening in the spiritual realm when this happens? Dark forces work overtime just behind the veil to convince you that your husband or wife is not the person for you, and that there is someone better out there. These are evil forces working through others to break up that which is sacred to God.

"So, they are no longer two, but one flesh. Therefore, what God has joined together, let no one separate." Matthew 19:6

I imagined the wife in the court case was probably in an affair with a professional man. Maybe even a man who was married and promising her that he'd get a divorce, too. Tears slowly started to roll down my cheeks, but I wiped them away quickly— I had to show strength. I said a prayer for the man, and in my thoughts, I condemned Satan and his evil spirits for breaking up that family.

Yet, instead of standing up and declaring that I wanted to stop this for my own marriage, I continued to sit there waiting for my turn to destroy my wife and break apart my family. Satan was happy. I pictured him wringing his hands in delight. His plan was coming together just the way he'd imagined.

Once the couple was done, the court secretary stood and said, "The Common Wealth of Kentucky now calls Julian Adkins as the petitioner, and Stephanie Adkins as the respondent."

I went and sat down in the seat of the "clinch-jawed woman of stone." Adjacent from me was my sweet bride of 31.5 years, sitting at the same table that the previous man in tears was seated. She was vulnerable, unprotected. I could tell this weighed heavy on her. *She has no family to be here to support her during this terrible event,* I thought.

Our wedding vows came to mind— I was the one who promised to protect her from that day forward. I was the one who was to shield her from these kinds of attacks, not put them on her.

To be honest, I didn't want to put her through this. I wanted to go and put my arms around her and tell her everything would be ok. But I had chosen this path, and I would be weak if I gave in. That's what the voices were saying. You know, the voices of friends, coworkers, and especially those in my social group in Florida.

My conscience wasn't saying anything, because I'd told it to shut up a long time ago.

The day ended with us determining that I would pay all the bills and provide child support for our teenage son. I was determined not to be known as a father who didn't support his family. Ironic, huh?

While still in Kentucky that following Sunday, I went to church. The Pastor spoke of how the world had changed. He went on to say, "Fathers are abandoning their families, when they should be the spiritual leader of their homes. Their hearts are growing cold toward their wives and families." I thought, *I'm such a coward. What kind of man leaves his family?* I was torn. Was the Pastor talking about me? 5,000 people attended our church; he couldn't be talking about me, right? I supported my family financially! He must be talking about someone else. *I completely ignored the spiritual aspect of supporting my family.* I was in denial of so much. The Lord was speaking truth into my soul through that Pastor, but I wouldn't listen.

The next day, as I was getting ready for the return trip to Florida, I received a text from my teenage son telling me that his mom, my soon-to-be divorced wife, was in the emergency room at a nearby hospital for heart issues. That call scared me. I thought, *I did this to her.*

I needed to go see her. I told myself, again, that I would always love her. She was the love of my youth, and the mother of our children.

There in the emergency room she was so fragile, so vulnerable. I could tell she was stressed. I had just seen her a few days before, crying in the courtroom, and saying that she couldn't do this, she couldn't discuss tearing apart our family.

In the emergency room, I held her hand and tried to comfort her. I told her everything was going to be all right. The visit seemed to calm and relax her. We talked a little, and later she was discharged.

Divorce Court: Take Two

The month of March had rolled around, and I had scheduled some spring-break time with my two younger children. I'd invited them to come to Florida to enjoy the sun with me, but they had conditions and demands: they wanted me to take them to Universal and Disney World. Funny, in an ironic sort of way. We planned for a week total— a few days at Universal, and a few days at the beach. I wanted, more than anything, to keep up a good relationship with my children, as well as my son-in-law, and grandson. My youngest two flew to Florida, and brought a friend in tow. There seemed to be a big elephant consistently with us. My children acted like they were happy, but I could tell, behind their smiling faces, they weren't. They were upset, and my son was very angry.

May was upon me, and I headed to Kentucky for court once again. Stephanie sat across from me, and I could tell she had been crying. The divorce proceedings were tearing her apart. I don't recall the exact reason for being in court that day, since it appeared that nothing was accomplished. Near the end of the session, the judge started a discussion on scheduling the final court date.

I began to think that the pattern of court appearances was about every two months. I thought, *our next court date will be on our anniversary in July, which will be horrible.* I didn't want that, and I knew Stephanie didn't either. The attorneys and the judge went back and forth a few times regarding availability, and the result inevitably landed on our anniversary date in late July. Stephanie gasped, about to break down in tears. Her attorney was observant enough to realize the importance of the date.

I leaned over to my attorney and voiced, "That date wouldn't work." She looked at me with big eyes and said, "Do you want to get divorced or what"? I whispered, "The date for our final court appearance is our anniversary." Before my attorney could suggest a different date, Stephanie's attorney blurted out that she wasn't available, and a new date in August was settled on.

I looked over at Stephanie; she was an emotional mess, completely devastated by the court event. I felt even worse. I started to question the divorce, and thought I would end up with the short end of the stick—both financially and emotionally. The sailboat was a pipe dream, and it was going up in smoke. The writing was on the wall. I would be left with the debt, my children would hate me for the rest of my life, and— worst of all— I would be losing the best thing that ever happened to me, *my wife*.

What was I doing?

As soon as doubt entered my mind, I pushed it away as quickly as I could.

Court was over, and I wanted to talk to Stephanie. Up to this point, we hadn't talked except for a few words. While in the parking lot, I texted her and asked if she would like to go out for lunch. She agreed, and we met somewhere local. I wanted to see how she was feeling, and to work out our differences on the terms of our divorce.

Because we had children, we would be in a relationship the rest of our lives, so we needed to agree on the divorce terms. We were still in conflict about selling our home. It was one of the big-ticket items of the divorce, and she wanted to remain in it until our son graduated high school. I wanted to sell it so we could pay debts and split the earnings and, of course, so I could buy my sailboat.

I should point out that Stephanie had been a stay-at-home mother since the birth of our first child, and she'd homeschooled all our children until they reached high school. She had no real job experience, yet I expected her to walk into the job market and make her own way.

While at lunch, Stephanie shared that she had started to pray over our home, going into each room to pray over them, claiming the entire house for our children and herself, in Jesus' name. I ignored her prayer. In my mind the divorce was still on, I just wanted us to be friends. We had a nice lunch that day, with good discussions about our children and grandchild. Overall, it was a move in a positive direction. The meeting was the planting of positive seeds, and I may not fully realize the outcome of those seeds for years to come.

Nonetheless, I went back to Florida in hopes of a better life, where every day was sunny. Where there were blue skies, no worries, and everybody was all smiles.

The Power of Prayer

Back in Florida, I joined a premier yacht club in Tampa and was racing sailboats two or three times a week. I was building relationships with other sailors who, like me, loved being on the water. I started to spend a lot of time with my sailing friends and became really close to an islander from Trinidad, named Ravi.

I found it interesting that many people who live in Florida are not natives of Florida. There are very few people who were born and raised in Florida. Ravi came to Florida after first entering the United States through New York. Later, he'd migrated south. Ravi was thin, had long dreadlocks, and looked about 20 years younger than he was. He had served in the military just like I had, so we had a brotherly bond. He and I got along great. He loved being on the water just as much as I did, and he had several sailboats of various types.

We made several sailing trips from the Hillsborough River, across Tampa Bay, to the Gulf Coast with some of our friends from the yacht club. We also had a few talks about the Lord, and Ravi believed just as I did. Like me, however, he wasn't practicing his faith in God.

Between the time of May, June, and July, Stephanie agreed on some dates for our teenaged son to visit with me in Tampa. Stephanie and I had joint custody during the divorce proceedings, and I wanted, more than anything, to have a relationship with my son. While he was staying with me, Stephanie wasn't far away in St. Petersburg, Florida, on a much-needed vacation from all the stress the last nine months had brought. Little did I know that my son had asked Stephanie to be nearby in case he needed her, and in case he wanted to end his visit with me. I knew he wasn't interested in visiting me, but Stephanie asked him to so that the pre-divorce custody agreement would be satisfied. I knew that my son was hurt and angry about the way I left the family.

Our son had been taking piano and voice lessons since he was nine years old. He's a natural performer and loves to sing pop, blues, and gospel songs, among many other genres. He was 15 years old at the time. Before his visit, I had arranged for him to play and sing at a local upscale Italian restaurant, while the jazz band was on break. Stephanie joined us, since this was our son and I wanted her to enjoy his successes as well.

He played the piano and sang wonderfully. He was super, and the restaurant crowd loved it. We were so proud of him, and I enjoyed having all three of us there at the same time. Again, this was a small seed I hoped would eventually grow into a mutual relationship around our children. Little did I realize the greater seed that was being planted.

The summer of 2017 was unique for sure. Stephanie came to St. Petersburg on another vacation in July. When near the shore, she loves going to the beaches and shell hunting, and she makes sunsets a highlight of every day. She will patiently watch the sunset in the evening, and enjoys the daily transformation as the sun goes down on the horizon. She particularly likes watching as the clouds change colors from red-orange, to bright pink, and then to various yellows.

We had made plans to meet for dinner while Stephanie was in Florida. Keep in mind, we had an August court date just around the corner where we would divide everything fifty-fifty and be officially divorced. I dreaded that final court date.

We met for dinner, and we sincerely enjoyed ourselves. In fact, dinner was so successful that we ended up spending more time together than initially planned. She had a couple of nights booked at Disney World and invited me to come for the day. I accepted the invitation. I could clearly see something was changing between us, and I wanted to explore the change to see if it was real. I hated going to Disney, and here's why: I have been to Disney over ten times, and Stephanie has been there more than twenty times. Whenever it was our family vacation time, Stephanie always voted that we should go to Disney, and she would win the support of our children each year. The places I wanted to go to were Mount Rushmore, The Grand Canyon, Niagara Falls, or Martha's Vineyard, but these places were always shot down and I was overruled. When I left Stephanie, I vowed that I would never go to Disney again.

During our time at Disney, she shared with me that she was seeking God and praying for our marriage. Up until four months prior, Stephanie had not been praying for our marriage. She'd been continually praying, but not for me.

She was just done with me. My actions as an unfaithful husband had caused her to lose hope and shut down. I thought our marriage wouldn't change, and so did she— but for different reasons. A part of her was ready to find a man who would truly honor, cherish, and be faithful to her— things I had failed to do.

One day, she sought God and asked what He would have her do concerning our marriage. She further explained that the Holy Spirit spoke to her heart and clearly said, "Pray for your marriage, but know free will is involved." She also shared with me that she had been praying a faith vision[1] over me and our marriage since March 2017.

This struck up a great conversation, since I wanted to know what exactly she was praying. One thing I knew for sure is that God answers prayer, and I wondered if my days in Florida were numbered. I was raised from childhood to know and understand the power of prayer— I had seen many answered prayers because of prayer warriors like my grandmothers, Caroline and Josephine, and my mother, Thelma. I knew that God honors those who are in good standing with Him and pray in faith. Prayer is power for the Christian, especially when you speak God's words over your situation.

---

[1] A faith vision is where you take God's Holy Scriptures and turn them into a prayer for those you love. I discuss this further, and provide examples, in a section in the back of the book called "Stephanie's Faith Vision".

I told Stephanie, "I'm in trouble." I said it jokingly, but in my heart, I knew that the Holy Spirit would be coming after me in full force, and with many angels behind Him, to do spiritual battle against those evil spirits that had subdued me and carried me away. I feared the sorrows that might be put into my path to help turn my heart back to God, my wife, and my family. It was a mystery to me how it all would work, but I knew that if she was praying, change would be coming soon.

Stephanie asked if she could read the faith vision to me. I didn't protest. Once she finished, I asked her to send it to me in a text, because I wanted to review it on my own later. That evening, while by myself, I started to read the prayer. Tears began flowing again as I read. Fundamentally, by reading the prayer, I was speaking God's Word over myself. I imagined God's angels fighting with evil demons in hand-to-hand combat for my soul, right there in my bedroom.

Later that evening, I met up with Stephanie again and we enjoyed the sunset together on the beach of Pass-A-Grille, Florida. I felt a renewed respect for her, and I began looking at her differently, because I could tell she was making an effort to keep us together.

We had a lot of fun that night. For the first time in a long time, we focused on us. We pushed our differences aside and just tried to enjoy each other while she was on vacation. There was a lot of respect going both ways. It wasn't my way or her way, our activities were based on a mutual agreement. We kept saying that this vacation should have been the vacation that failed in 2016.

She asked what I thought about the faith vision. Because I know the power of prayer, I said to her, "I guess things will be changing for me soon." After Stephanie went back home to Kentucky, I felt differently about her. I had prayed many times, asking God to help me through this divorce situation. Was my heart changing about Stephanie? Had it changed enough to turn me around?

I felt compelled to extend the court date from August to September, and perhaps give us more time. We were about two weeks from our August court date. I emailed my attorney and asked if we could extend the court date out a month. I didn't believe the judge would simply allow me to extend the court date, but it couldn't hurt to ask.

My attorney replied, "The Judge is asking why?" I replied, "Divorce is a colossal decision, and I want to be sure it is the right thing to do." A few days later, my attorney emailed that the divorce date was extended per my request. Fortunately, the new date was rescheduled to November, 2017.

At this point, I felt I was on the fence about the divorce, and believed November would give me adequate time to make a final decision. I found that Stephanie's communication with her attorney wasn't as instantaneous as mine was with my attorney, because about a week out from the August court date, she texted me saying, "You moved our court date to November?"

Meanwhile, still in Florida, I continued a search to find something to make me feel happy. I felt pressed as I tossed my options around in my mind. I listened to all the voices, and now I felt the smoke was clearing. The storm from my dream was close to being over, and I could think more precisely now. I could feel something in me was scrambling, scratching, trying to say, "NO! You've come too far to turn back now."

I kept thinking that I didn't want to be by myself after the divorce, I just wasn't the type of person that could live the rest of my life alone. On the other hand, I didn't want to get married again, and I loved the fact that Stephanie and I saw eye-to-eye regarding our faith. When I looked at the social groups I was involved in, I found that none of the women in those groups believed the Bible like I did. I looked at the yacht club and saw women who loved to sail, but I could immediately tell that sailing was their god. I wanted someone who believed in the Bible as I did.

Maybe Stephanie was my wife for a far greater purpose than I could see? Imagine that!

One day at church, I felt the Holy Spirit reprimand me for even thinking about pulling one of His precious daughters into a divorce debacle.

Still, I was compartmentalizing what the Bible said about divorce and ignoring the warnings. God hates divorce, but Satan loves it, because he is the opposite of God. There's no in-between.

"'I hate divorce,' says the Lord, the God of Israel..." Malachi 2:16 (NLT)

Someone once told me, concerning God and His Truth, "There must be an in-between, or somewhere in the middle." No, there is no middle road.

"No one can serve two masters. Either you hate the one and love the other, or you will be devoted to the one and despise the other. You cannot serve both God and money [Satan]." Matthew 6:24

I bracketed "Satan" because 1 Timothy 6:10 states that the root of all kinds of evil is money, and we know Satan is where the root grows.

"For the love of money is a root of all kinds of evil, for which some have strayed from the faith in their greediness, and pierced themselves through with many sorrows." 1 Timothy 6:10 (NKJV)

The woman I was most compatible with lived in Kentucky. She was the same woman that had been set aside for me from the beginning of time. She was the same woman that my dad had seen as a little girl, running around in her grandparent's General Store in Richwood, Kentucky, as he stopped the locomotive train to deliver limestone. She was the same woman for whom, during my senior year in high school, I had deliberately missed eating lunch, just so I could go meet her in the gymnasium and share the orange that she brought with her lunch. The same woman that had followed me across the United States and overseas during my Army career. She was the same woman who was called by God to homeschool our children. She poured all of herself into our children and their education as she relentlessly homeschooled them over the years.

The same woman who was wholeheartedly dedicated to our marriage.

September rolled around, and I was thinking about the great time Stephanie and I had together in July. I texted her one day and asked if she would like to go to New York together, because we'd had so much fun while in St. Petersburg. I wanted to see if it was a fluke, or if we would have a good time again. She said she would have to think about it. So, I didn't get a solid answer from her, yet she was the woman that would keep me wanting more.

Chapter 3

The Prodigal Husband

Storm clouds hovered in the atmosphere, both literally and figuratively. Hurricane Irma spun over Miami, Florida on a northwesterly trek and turned, spinning toward Tampa. Just as that storm passed, another one struck. Remember my housemate, Jack? He and I shared the three-bedroom condo for almost a year while I was in Florida. We didn't spend much time together because we had differing views about a lot of things, and we were both working through issues; he was struggling with bouncing from job to job after a successful career in insurance sales; I, of course, had the divorce. I think the only thing that we agreed about were a few political views, our desires for a free and easy Florida lifestyle, and that staying in a relationship with our children was one of the most important things we could do as fathers.

One Friday evening in mid-September, I attended a meeting at the beach in St. Pete— one of the first social gatherings I attended after hurricane Irma hit Florida. I returned from the beach just after midnight. Pulling onto my street, I found police tape and other official barriers blocking the road. I parked on an adjacent street and walked toward the front of my condo. I asked the police officer monitoring the road if I could go inside my house. He nodded, so I went in. I was tired, but was anxious to see if

Jack knew anything about why the police had blocked off this section of our neighborhood. I would typically find him sitting on the couch watching the news or his favorite Netflix series, and his Saturdays were typically spent with fellow boaters, out fishing on a 40-foot powerboat in the bay.

Upon entering the condo, I checked the garage on the first floor and I found it strange that Jack's truck wasn't there. I expected to see Jack the next day, but he still wasn't around— and there was no evidence that he'd come home the night before. I knocked on his bedroom door, but there was no response.

On Sunday, after church, I headed down to the yacht club on Davis Island for a sailing event. While at the event, I overheard someone mention the police being at our yacht club community on Friday night. I listened intently and jumped into the conversation to ask what it was all about. The person told me that Jack had shot and killed a man. I was astonished!

It suddenly made sense why he had not been home since Friday evening. I drove straight to the police station to get the full story of what had happened.

As you can imagine, being told that your housemate killed a man causes all kinds of thoughts and questions to run through your mind. The officer at the police station told me that he couldn't share anything about the incident except that Jack allegedly shot a man in the street nine times. I was utterly baffled by the news.

Although Jack wasn't an entirely terrible housemate, we'd had a few disagreements over the past year. I could always tell he had a short fuse, and I'd preferred to keep my distance.

I thought about the man he shot, and wondered if it could have been me. The whole situation with Jack stirred the pot; my fun-filled, luxury living promptly became a less ideal situation. I was forced to find a place of my own now that I couldn't share a condo with Jack, and it would cost me double, if not triple, what I was previously paying.

I went to talk with a real estate manager about the situation. Come to find out, Jack did not own the condo we lived in. The owner asked me to move out immediately, because he wanted to lock the place up until after Jack's murder case went to court.

I explained that I would need at least a month to find a home and make adjustments. He offered me a surprising amount of money if I agreed to move out in two weeks. I hit the streets, looking for a place to live in alone. Stephanie and I talked a lot more since her visits to Florida, so I kept her updated about my situation.

My house hunt turned up nothing but poor results. The areas I was forced to consider were not the luxury standard to which I grown accustomed, and the possibility of finding a place of my own grew grim.

The next day, things moved fast. I found a place for rent near the water in St. Petersburg that wasn't too bad. The rent was going to stretch me, to say the least— especially when I considered what I would be paying in child support and maintenance. My confidence in the situation had hit an all-time low. I felt like a boat adrift, and land was nowhere in sight. The reality of my situation, versus the life I thought I could live, was rapidly becoming clearer.

    I went to a leasing office in St. Petersburg and paid a deposit to start the application process. Done with that, I headed back to the car. Strangely, on a sunny day with no clouds in the sky, a rain cloud seemed to appear out of nowhere and pass directly overhead. My phone rang as I was getting into my car— it was the leasing office telling me I had the green light to move into the 2-bedroom apartment. Just seconds later, raindrops the size of grapes began to fall.

    It was a beautiful sunny day, and for large rain drops to fall in such a concentrated area was peculiar.

    In fact, it was raining so hard I couldn't see enough to drive. I just sat in my car with time to think about my situation. Just as I'd done many, many times before, I thought about the big picture of my failing marriage, and how it would impact me and my family the rest of my life. I thought about how I had hurt the love of my life and my children with such deep suffering, and how that pain wasn't going to go away anytime soon.

    I would probably never get to know my grandson. My heart sank at the thought.

    I wasn't happy, and I wouldn't be satisfied anytime soon if I continued down this broad path of sin and destruction. As I continued to sit there, with the rain pelting the roof of my car, I heard the Holy Spirit say in that still, quiet voice, "You will have to humble yourself, and your pride will need to take a back seat. Go home to your wife. Go home to your family".

Tears ran down my face again. I felt defeated. I couldn't do anything right. I couldn't even be successful in leaving my family. Weeping seemed to be a common thing for me, lately.

The Holy Spirit reminded me of the story of the prodigal son. I said out loud in the car, "Oh great, I guess I'm the prodigal husband?"

He showed me the comparison of how I thought I lived in one of the most esteemed communities, but how, in reality, I was living with a bunch of pigs in one giant pig pen. The Holy Spirit showed me the life I had been living was a paradigm to the prodigal son, and it was time I went home to the Father.

He was right; I could see the comparison of my desires for living in a community of big boats, expensive cars, expensive houses, beautiful women, and all the luxuries of life a person could ever want, to the desires of the foolish prodigal son. And just like the prodigal son's situation, my life was changing.

I was nearly homeless, and if I didn't start making the right decisions, I *would* be homeless very soon. I began to pray, and I simply talked to God as if He was sitting beside me. We were both sitting there, waiting for the little rain cloud, hovering over my car out of nowhere, to pass. I told

Him about how imperfect I was. I confessed what an idiot I was. The Holy Spirit agreed with me. I asked Him to forgive me for all my wrong turns, and I asked Him how many times I would have to go through stuff like this. His reply was, "When you decide to stop making poor choices." I probably sat there for an hour or more.

When I was done praying, having that one-on-one conversation with my Creator, the rain stopped. The sun shone brightly. Thinking back, I find it interesting that the rain kept intensifying until I prayed the prayer of repentance. I started the car and pulled away as I made a phone call.

From the time it took to go from the real estate office and allow a rainstorm to pass, I came to the conclusion that I was packing everything up and moving back to Kentucky.

Stephanie answered the phone and asked how the house hunting was going. I explained that I'd found a place to live and had just put down $100 for a background check. Then I asked if she would take me back and was willing to forgive me. She said it wouldn't be easy, and that we would need to take it slow and go through the right process to ensure we were grounded moving forward. I agreed with her, I wanted to be grounded as well. I asked her why she would want me back after everything I had done to her and our children. Her response was simple, yet powerful, **"It really has nothing to do with who you are right now. It has everything to do with God and who I am in Christ."**

She also told me I could not move back into our home until she saw I was serious about rebuilding our marriage.

That weekend, I packed up my car and went back to Kentucky— with a humble heart and my pride in check. My good friend, Ravi, made the drive with me to keep me company, and he flew back to Tampa after a couple of days.

Shortly after my return to Kentucky, since we'd had so much fun together during Stephanie's vacation in Florida, we decided to move forward with our planned 4-day trip to New York City. I still had reservations about getting back together, and I wasn't entirely sure what the future held for us. I wasn't sure we *could* get back together— the enemy wouldn't stop placing doubts in my mind. But I knew how big my God was, and I knew He could heal any and every marriage, if I were willing to take the steps toward restoration that He prescribed.

Our court date was still set for early November, and it was October when we traveled to the Big Apple for the first time in our lives. Local weathermen reported the temperature of those four days in October as the warmest since the 1800's. The days were beautiful, with sunny blue skies and warm temperatures. We enjoyed walks in Central Park, in the company of one another.

Stephanie is good at understanding the subway systems in large cities, such as Frankfurt, Germany, and Paris, France. She'd proved that her subway transportation skills were top notch, so we used public transportation to get around. We treated each other with respect and rediscovered "*us*" during those days. We attended Hillsong Church and enjoyed New York-style pizza while in Hell's Kitchen. We visited the Statue of Liberty, and took a convertible bus tour of the city that turned into a time of sunshine, laughter, and new experiences. We had so much fun that I asked myself, *what happened to us over the years, and how did we become so disconnected?* We both relaxed and talked about our future while discovering the city together.

Not long after our return from New York, we decided that I would move back into our family home. We were still on very shaky ground, with so much work needing to be done— but we wanted to make it work. Our children were not as excited about the prospect, especially our oldest and youngest. I had put them through so much, and they were not as easily forgiving. Not only did I hurt and betray them, but they saw first-hand the pain I'd put their mother through.

Once back home, Stephanie and I started to attend church together. After service, I asked if she wanted to go to one of the prayer team couples for prayer. She later told me she was astonished when I said I wanted to go up for prayer. Previously, my pride would keep me from going up for prayer, because I never wanted anyone to think I was troubled or needed help. But now I had surrendered to God. I was done running, it was time to start rebuilding the mess

I had made. It was time to start rebuilding our marriage and to make it stronger than ever before.

At the front of the church, before God and the congregation, I asked Jesus, once again, to forgive me for all my wrongdoings. I immediately felt a hefty load lifted from my shoulders as we prayed for our marriage. The feeling was similar to when you are building something, assembling the pieces, and every piece clicks perfectly into place.

Imagine assembling a large structure and finding a bind in the components while you're joining the parts together, making everything not fit together properly. When we prayed that night, it felt like the final piece, the one I had been looking for all my life, was moved into position. All the load-bearing structures were suddenly balanced. I felt a spiritual "click", as if something fell into place.

On the way home that night, I knew our marriage had a long, painful road ahead of us. Patching this up wouldn't be easy, there were a lot of hurts on both sides, but we believed the promise that with God, all things are possible (Matthew 19:26). We started discussions about going to a marriage counselor.

Knowing how much I hurt Stephanie and my children is a tremendous burden that I think about often, and it lays heavy on my heart. Occasionally, I have to cry out to God to lighten my load, because the guilt is simply too much to bear.

Satan and his discouraging band of evil doubters would try to tell me that it was going to be too hard to reconcile, and that I should give up. Thankfully, the Holy Spirit reached down and pulled me out of that depressing slump every time. With His grace, I'd focus and say, "Not today Satan, get thee behind me!!"

Later, our church provided us with an extensive list of marriage counselors. I prayed over the list and asked the Holy Spirit to guide us to the right one. However, we weren't getting any positive word from the Lord. Then, one evening, a friend from our small group invited us to a *Married for Life* Outreach, which is a 2=1 International ministry based in Colorado. At the Outreach we found a broad spectrum of married couples, young and old. Those that wanted a more intimate walk with Christ to bring their marriage in line with Scripture, couples that needed direction and purpose, and lastly, couples that needed a Godly intervention, otherwise they may not last through the week.

Stephanie and I had already decided to get back together, so we felt that we were hopefully past the intervention stage, but we desperately needed direction and purpose. I could hear the Holy Spirit tell me in a calm, yet stern, voice, "This is it! I want you and Stephanie to enroll". Stephanie and I both agreed that the Lord was directing us to this *Married for Life* course.

With one week to spare, the divorce proceedings were canceled with the county court. My attorney emailed me when it was finalized, saying that the judge was pleased that we were working on our marriage, and not becoming another statistic.

Chapter 4

The First Step is Obedience

The *Married for Life* course was a small group of about seven couples that would meet for roughly two hours a week for twelve weeks. Each week would build on the previous week, teaching the couples God's view on marriage.

Once we started the *Married for Life* course, I sat next to my wife listening to the leaders teach us the content ordained by the Holy Spirit, while He was simultaneously whispering in my ear. When the Holy Spirit started talking to me in his gentle, loving, constructive way, I became a sobbing mess. I was in tears for almost the entire class that evening. The other couples must have thought I was one of the most emotional men they had ever seen. I was crying all the time, even during breaks. He was showing me the right way to love my wife, my children, and how to be a respectful husband and father. I saw all the mistakes I'd made, and I wanted to do it right this time.

The Holy Spirit started to give me vivid images, visions, and dreams like never before. He had spoken to me many times through the years in the same manner, but my prior visions and dreams were few and far between, scattered over forty years. Past spiritual experiences weren't as intensified and concentrated on a specific subject like marriage, as it was now.

He provided a rundown of everything we had been through in the last two years, and during our painful divorce process—but this time from a spiritual perspective. Through an open vision (my eyes were open and seeing a motion picture of another place and time, and at the same time I could understand what was happening in the present), He showed me how marriage was a castle, blessed by God from the moment a man and woman say, "I Do." When a couple exchanges marital vows, God transforms their marriage into a mighty fortress that sits, guarded, on high ground in the spiritual realm. Fundamentally, marriages are a strong, undeniable fortress supported directly by God.

He also pointed out that there has never been a castle built in the history of man that could ultimately withstand the forces of evil without God's help. Essentially, when a man and woman are united in marriage and unified in Christ, then God is the fortress, and the marriage dwells within Him. He showed me this through a vision, and brought Psalm 46:7 to mind:

"The LORD Almighty is with us; the God of Jacob is our fortress." Psalm 46:7

On the opposing side of this fascinating discovery, was the fact that those couples who do not claim Jesus as their Lord have cause for alarm in the spiritual realm. Their inherited lands, their bounty, and their castle structure are open to be afflicted, attacked, defeated, and— ultimately— destroyed.

The Holy Spirit spoke to me and said, "Julian, you have been trespassing against My institution of marriage and have sinned against My precepts. Now, let me show you how precious it is to Me." Then He started showing me the fortress, *The Marital Castle*.

He confirmed once again that Genesis 1:27-28 was His accurate model for marriage, and any other combination was a concoction from the father of all lies.

"So, God created mankind in his own image, in the image of God he created them; male and female he created them. God blessed them and said to them, 'Be fruitful and increase in number; fill the earth and subdue it. Rule over the fish in the sea and the birds in the sky and over every living creature that moves on the ground.'" Genesis 1:27-28

I make no apologies for the message in God's Word. Jesus tells us in several examples that many are offended by hearing God's Word (Luke 7:23). This is because it conflicts with our God-given free will and the desires of the flesh. Furthermore, the enemy has convinced many that the Scriptures were meant for a different time, therefore many find it abrasive and hard to digest. If you find yourself thinking that God's Word is offensive, then consider that you may have been fooled by the enemy of your soul.

The Spirit of God also showed me Paul's comment in Ephesians where he said,

"I pray that the eyes of your heart may be enlightened in order that you may know the hope to which he has called you..."
Ephesians 1:18

By opening my spiritual eyes, I plainly saw that because of my actions and the pride of life (1 John 2:16), I allowed the enemy's evil forces to bind me, gag me, blindfold me, and carry me away from my marital castle. In the vision, I saw how the enemy carried me away to a sandbar, and how the demons built a fire and started to dance around it in celebration as I lay bound on the sand.

The Holy Spirit then said to me, "You are to write a book concerning all that has happened with your marriage, and what I have shown you about the Marital Castle. I want others to see and understand this concept".

I confess that I protested. Fear overcame me, and my heart felt faint. I really didn't want to throw my sins in front of the world; to peel back the layers of my mistakes for all to see. I worried how opening up this can of worms would affect my family. Would they be embarrassed? When I told Stephanie that the Holy Spirit wanted me to publish a book about us, she wasn't on board either. The wounds of the past two years were still too fresh for her. It wasn't until I started the sixth chapter that she told me she was all in.

In the beginning, I was very reluctant and pushed back. I said, "Lord, I'm not the person to write a book about marriage. Our marriage came within a week of being legally broken, and I've set the worst example for any husband to follow." I asked many times, "Are You sure You chose the right person for this task?"

"Yes," The Holy Spirit consistently replied, as if He was saying, "I'm not taking 'no' for an answer."

"But I'm not a writer, I have no idea what I'm doing. It won't be perfect."

"Do you think the ark that Noah built was perfect?" He replied, "I had to fill in the gaps many times and I'll do the same for you."

It doesn't matter who you are, putting yourself and all your mistakes on a stage for all to see is really humiliating, and incredibly humbling. By agreeing to be obedient to the Holy Spirit, I would essentially be stepping off the curb of secular thinking and right in front of a spiritual bus. The bus would run me over, but He assured me I would live through it. He said, "Stick with Me, and you'll become an overcomer."

So, in March of 2018, I used my spare time to start writing what I wanted to put in the book. I wrote over 150 pages— approximately 30,000 words— of content through 2018. Finally, in January of 2019, the Holy Spirit said, "Thanks for writing everything you did. It was a good practice session, but that's not what I want in the book."

He began to lay out the content of this book in a vision— everything from the cover and chapters, to the castle analogy— along with various components of marriage, to match the structure of the castle. He also showed me the steps I would take to introduce the book, and that I was to have it done by October 2019.

The Holy Spirit led me in developing each chapter of this book, describing components of the Marital Castle, and how our testimony and this analogy would save marriages. The organization of the chapters and subchapters may not be what you would typically find in a book, but that is because the Holy Spirit instructed me to organize the ten chapters and include the subchapters as I have them in *The Marital Castle*.

The Holy Spirit was very adamant about the book being published by October 1st. I asked the Lord "Why October?" He said, "The new year will bring many blessings, and I will be doing a new thing. I will pour out My Spirit on My people like never before in the history of the earth." I was confused about October being the new year. He reiterated, "This book must be written before the new year (2020)." It was January 2019, so I thought, *I have plenty of time.* He then said, "Not by your time, but by Mine. Look at a Jewish calendar." I then realized the new year, by God's standards, was October 1st, 2019.

I asked the Lord about the book cover and where I would get the talent to provide dynamic art. I came up with some ideas of finding young talent from local schools, but they were not successful.

The idea about the art for the book cover had been weighing heavily on my mind, and I felt I needed to figure it out soon. I had been praying about it on and off for a few weeks.

One day, while driving with a friend to a prophetic conference in Tennessee, my friend's phone rang. The Holy Spirit said to me, "The person on the phone has your book cover in her head."

It was none of my business to ask who he was talking to, but I needed to find out who my book cover artist was. When he got off the call, he said, "Sorry about that, that was my daughter." I said, "It sounded like you had a pleasant conversation. Just out of curiosity, what does she do for a living?" He replied that she was very creative and owned her own art business! Before I knew it, I was talking to my book cover artist, and we had created a plan to work together on my project.

I could feel in my spirit that there was an urgency in this book matter. The Lord showed me how the book would start out— as a small kindling in a campfire, and quickly grow into a forest fire. He said, "You and Stephanie are to take your story to the church." I said, "Lord, these ministers aren't going to let some guy off the street speak to their congregations." He answered, very sternly, "You let me worry about that." Moving forward and being obedient would stretch me, but I said, "Yes, Lord, I am Your servant."

Finally, the Holy Spirit asked, "Did you not say, Here I am Lord?"

The Holy Spirit started to wake me during the early morning and would literally say, "Come spend some time with Me" Being tired, I would lay there and start to pray, but it wasn't long before I'd fall back to sleep. Later, I'd feel guilty for not getting up with Him. I felt like Jesus was coming to me the same way He went to the disciples in the early morning hours of Mathew 26:36-45, just before He was turned over to be crucified. He asked them to spend time with Him in prayer, but their eyes were heavy and they fell back to sleep. I felt the same way.

However, during the times that I obeyed the Holy Spirit, He gave me images and visions that the message in this book was **urgent**! Imagine warning signals, sirens sounding, and lights flashing that this is **urgent!** The urgency burned through me and was my motivational fuel.

The message is this: **Spiritual attacks on marriages are going to intensify in the very near future, and the Lord wants His people, those that have ears and understand the signs of the times, to be warned. He wants all marriages to be in line with Him and have the right tools to defend themselves against imminent attacks**.

The Lord spoke to my heart and said, "I want to restore My covenant and mercy with My people, and I want to shake those who are spiritually sleeping." This message was repeated for months. When truth and wisdom speak, obedience is compliant, so I decided to stop struggling and be obedient.

After Stephanie and I successfully completed our first *Married for Life* course, we felt the Lord leading us to go through the "Joshua training" to become *Married for Life* coaches. I recall our children commenting that it was crazy; less than a year ago we were on the county's family court docket for divorce proceedings, and now we were training to help other married couples find their God-given tools to make the right decisions about their future. The Holy Spirit said, "Look at examples in My Word. I've taken some of the worst sinners and transformed them for My purpose." Wow! He sure does know how to make the tears flow. I was so humbled. I decided; *I'm not going to blow this opportunity to do something for Him that truly matters.*

The Holy Spirit continued to wake me up in the early morning, around 3-5 am. I would get up half of the time, and I felt the Holy Spirit wasn't pleased with that. If He, the God of the universe, or even one of His mighty angels, was trying to get me up to pray, I wanted to be proactive. I started to hear the word "obedience" over and over, so I finally set my alarm clock for 4 AM.

I started to routinely get up and worship Him on my knees. I prayed, read His powerful word, and practiced being still (Psalm 46:10) in the quiet of the early morning, listening for direction. There were some nights when, before I went to bed, I would hear the Holy Spirit say, "In the morning, when you wake up, there will be a great spiritual breakthrough".

I was always anxious to get started. I could feel the warfare that was taking place in my spirit. Feeling the Holy Spirit on me to this extent was something I hadn't felt before; it felt like my blood was racing through my veins, but my heart wasn't doing the pumping. All my emotions and senses were in overdrive. On those nights, I almost couldn't fall asleep. Before long, I didn't even have to set my alarm clock. Somehow, I always woke at the top of the hour, between 3 and 5 am.

If the Holy Spirit is waking you in the early morning hours, it's because He wants your attention, and I believe the enemy forces are easily defeated during that time. It's a sweet blessing to know that the God of the Universe is waking you up to pray and worship Him. When He talks to you, it is so rewarding and overwhelming. I discuss this a little more in chapter nine, where I'll give you other Biblical examples of how battles were won during the "fourth watch."

"And blessed is he who is not offended because of Me." Luke 7:23 (NKJV)

"But mark this: There will be terrible times in the last days. People will be lovers of themselves, lovers of money, boastful, proud, abusive, disobedient to their parents, ungrateful, unholy, without love, unforgiving, slanderous, without self-control, brutal, not lovers of the good, treacherous, rash,

conceited, lovers of pleasure rather than lovers of God—having a form of godliness but denying its power. Have nothing to do with such people." 2 Timothy 3:1-5

"'In the last days,' God says, 'I will pour out my Spirit on all people. Your sons and daughters will prophesy, your young men will see visions, your old men will dream dreams. Even on my servants, both men and women, I will pour out my Spirit in those days, and they will prophesy.'" Acts 2:17

Prayer Time

The Lord started to wake me more and more during the early morning, which I reference as the fourth watch. My worship time during the fourth watch had become incredibly powerful, and I wanted to share it with you as an example. Please don't think this is the way your prayer time needs to be. This technique works for me, and I feel these steps helped me find an intimate relationship with Him. I encourage you to seek the Lord for guidance in how your prayer time should look.

I've listed seven steps that I attempt to follow while in my secret place with the Lord. In the next paragraph are some scriptures supporting those steps.

1. I always start my worship in a quiet place on my knees, especially during the fourth watch. To me, this is a physical display of being submissive and reverent before God. (Psalm 95:6)
2. I recite the Lord's Prayer. This prayer is a great way to start the day, even if it's at 3 or 4 am. (Matthew 6:9-13)
3. I play worship music on my phone at a low volume, so as not to wake the others in the house. I let praise and worship fill the atmosphere. Then I'll move into worshipping and singing. Before long, I start to feel the Holy Spirit hover over me. Typically, the room is pitch black during worship, and I sense He is in the place with me, along with His angels. (Psalm 95:1)
4. I'll praise God and acknowledge that He is holy and righteous. (Isaiah 6:3)
5. I start praying about general concerns. I like to mention it all, in detail. The scripture that rings in my ear when I petition the Lord is, "You have not

because you ask not" (James 4:2). I make sure to cover the details. The Word tells us that prayer is powerful. (James 5:16, Philippians 4:6)

*I continue to pray and worship Him until I feel there is a breakthrough. (Ephesians 6:18)

6. If I have faith visions (statements made up using scripture), I'll speak those aloud. By speaking His Word, it becomes a two-edged sword. (Hebrews 4:12)
7. I read my daily devotion and study His Word. (Psalm 119:105 and Matthew 4:4)

Supporting Scriptures

1. "Come, let us bow down in worship, let us kneel before the LORD, our Maker." Psalm 95:6
2. "This, then, is how you should pray:
'Our Father in heaven, hallowed be your name, your kingdom come, your will be done, on earth as it is in heaven. Give us today our daily bread. And forgive us our debts, as we also have forgiven our debtors. And lead us not into temptation, but deliver us from the evil one.'" Matthew 6:9-13
3. "Come, let us sing for joy to the LORD; let us shout aloud to the Rock of our salvation." Psalm 95-1
4. "...Holy, holy, holy is the LORD Almighty; the whole earth is full of his glory." Isaiah 6:3
5. "...You do not have because you do not ask God." James 4:2
"Do not be anxious about anything, but in every situation, by prayer and petition, with thanksgiving, present your requests to God." Philippians 4:6
"Ask and it will be given to you; seek and you will find; knock, and the door will be opened to you. For everyone who asks receives; the one who seeks finds;

and to the one who knocks, the door will be opened. Which of you, if your son asks for bread, will give him a stone? Or if he asks for a fish, will give him a snake? If you, then, though you are evil, know how to give good gifts to your children, how much more will your Father in heaven give good gifts to those who ask him!" Matthew 7:7-10

"And pray in the Spirit on all occasions with all kinds of prayers and requests. With this in mind, be alert and always keep on praying for all the Lord's people." Ephesians 6:18

6. *"For the word of God is alive and active. Sharper than any double-edged sword, it penetrates even to dividing soul and spirit, joints and marrow; it judges the thoughts and attitudes of the heart." Hebrews 4:12*

7. *"Your word is a lamp to my feet and a light on my path." Psalm 119:105*

   "It is written: 'Man shall not live on bread alone, but on every word that comes from the mouth of God.'" Matthew 4:4

Chapter 5

Marital Foundations

Stephanie's Marital Foundations

Stephanie's maternal and paternal grandparents lived a mere three miles apart. Both of her lineages stretch back to some of the first settlers in Northern Kentucky. Her maternal great-grandparents attended one of the oldest churches in the county named Richwood Presbyterian. Stephanie later attended Richwood Presbyterian as a fourth-generation member, and her family was significantly involved in church activities there.

Her maternal grandparents were farmers and small-business owners. They had tobacco farms, a community store, a coal business, and rental properties. Her grandparents eventually bought property in Florida in the late 1960s, near Debary. They'd go to Florida for the winter, and come back to Kentucky for the summers. Stephanie was very close to her grandparents.

Her paternal grandparents lived across the street from the Richwood Presbyterian church, but attended a Nazarene church. Stephanie has fond memories of walking into her grandmother's home and seeing her Mama (grandmother) reading the Bible, interceding in prayer for her family. To this day, Stephanie believes there has been a protective covering over her life, and she attributes it to her grandmother's prayers.

Stephanie's parents, Don and Bonnie, were from a small, rural town in Northern Kentucky— the kind of town where everyone knows everyone. It was Don's friendship with Bonnie's older brother that really brought them together. Stephanie often says that her father and uncle were real rascals who had a knack for finding trouble. Don and Bonnie were married in 1957. They had three children, Stephanie being the youngest, before they divorced after sixteen years of marriage. Stephanie was just eight years old at the time of the divorce, but she still has very vivid memories of those turbulent times. She knew that when she got married, she wanted it to be for life.

In 2019, while Stephanie and her mother were on vacation in Florida, Bonnie shared, for the first time that, in 1959 Don had dropped her and their oldest child at his parent's farm to do laundry. That night, Don never returned. Several weeks went by before Bonnie found out— via a third party— that Don had left them and driven to South Florida. Don returned to Kentucky about a year later, and Stephanie was born several years later. Sadly, the two most important men in Stephanie's life had followed the same path.

I mysteriously followed her father's footsteps, leaving his family for a life in Florida— and I had no idea I was repeating the curse.

*"The L*ORD *is longsuffering and abundant in mercy, forgiving iniquity and transgression; but He by no means clears the guilty, <u>visiting the iniquity of the fathers on the children to the third and fourth generation.</u>" Numbers 14:18 (NKJV, emphasis added)*

Julian's Marital Foundations

My paternal grandfather, James, was from Christiansburg, Virginia. He started serving the Lord early in his life and married his wife, Josephine, at a very young age. He was a coal miner at age fourteen, and retired from the coal mines when he was thirty-four. After retirement, he dedicated his life to serving the Lord. James and Josephine joined a small group of like-minded believers who wanted to spread the gospel into remote areas in the Appalachian Mountains. They both became missionaries on horseback to accomplish their calling. James and Josephine would later work closely with the Church of God (COG) ministries in Cleveland, Tennessee. Today, this ministry has over 7 million members in 185 countries (Church of God, 2019).

James was an excellent carpenter, and he had a knack for building and starting churches. Not only did he build churches, James held tent revivals and regular services at least three times a week. Josephine was always by his side, masterfully playing the piano at each service. Their family grew. Over the years, they would move their daughter and three sons to multiple places— as far south as Louisiana, as far west as Kansas, and as far north as Pennsylvania, just south of the Canadian border. They would usually live in places provided by local members of the church. Sometimes that meant living with another family, in a dilapidated house, or an old trailer.

Today, many locations where James and Josephine planted churches are no farther than twelve hours away from where we live. Back before expressways, however, these locations may have been a couple days' drive from each other. My grandparents uprooted their family every few years (or less), packed up all they owned, and moved to unfamiliar places. James and Josephine dedicated their entire lives, and their family, to the selfless service of ministering the gospel of Jesus Christ wherever the Holy Spirit led them.

My father, also named Julian, was the second of four kids. In 1957, James and Josephine moved to Clarksville, Pennsylvania, to help build up a congregation there. Their three oldest children had already moved out on their own, so they had only their youngest son in tow. My father was living in Newport, Kentucky, at the time, but he moved to Clarksville, Pennsylvania in January of 1959 in search of a job. There, he joined his parents and baby brother in the little white church parsonage attached to the rear of the church.

On Sunday, January 18th, 1959, my dad, Julian, met my mom, Thelma, at the small Pentecostal Church of God in Clarksville, Pennsylvania. My dad preached that Sunday, and while he was preaching the Holy Spirit pointed out his spouse-to-be, who was sitting in the congregation. After church service that day, Julian asked Thelma out on a date. At the same time, he communicated that the Holy Spirit had told him that she was going to be his wife. She jokingly replied, "Well, the Holy Spirit hasn't shared that with me, and no, I'm not going out with you."

It turned out that Julian and Thelma would spend the next couple of weeks getting to know one another before James joined together his son, Julian, and his new daughter-in-law, Thelma, in a wedding ceremony on Monday, February 2nd, 1959— in the same church they'd met in. They knew each other for precisely sixteen days before saying, "I Do." Now that's a leap of faith!

They had seven children, thirty-six grandchildren, thirty-four great-grandchildren, and two great-great-grandchildren. They went on to build an incredible legacy together. In August 2018— and just a few months shy of being married sixty years- Julian passed away at 81 years of age.

I have written about my maternal grandparents in chapter six, *"Farming your Relationships"*.

Personal Spiritual Foundations

Stephanie's Spiritual Foundations

Stephanie was raised in a small rural town, primarily by her mother. Her parents divorced when she was eight years old, so she spent a lot of time between grandparents and extended family members. When her mother couldn't take her to church, her aunt would pick her up. Thanks to her aunt's involvement in her life, Stephanie was an active member of her church, and involved in various ministries. When she tells her salvation story, she acknowledges that her church taught about following God, loving Jesus, and living a good life; but she doesn't recall anyone ever telling her that she had to repent of her sins.

Stephanie and I started to date when we were 17 years old. She regularly attended church with me, and within a couple of months she asked Christ to be the Lord of her life. She was already living the life, but that confession of faith placed a seal of God's love over her heart forever.

Julian's Spiritual Foundations

I said, "Here I am, Lord" one Sunday night when my pastor preached on serving God. I remember accurately who was preaching, where we were, and what was preached. Sunday nights were a great time to rest under the wooden bench pews (while counting the pieces of gum stuck on the bottom of the seat) and listen to God's word being delivered.

You see, I was nine years old when I said, "Here I am Lord, I accept the challenge." I remember it like it was yesterday.

I listened intently to Pastor Daugherty preach at the Crescent Springs Church of God, where my family attended and my Dad was my Children's Church pastor. Pastor Daugherty said, "All of us have a calling on our life," and then he asked, "What is your calling? What has God called you to do for Him?" The message pulled at my heart and called me to action. I wanted to do something for the Lord. Even as a child, I knew it might not be something that I wouldn't want to do, but I was willing to take that step. I sat up on the edge of the pew and listened intently.

There are many passages in the Bible that command all to be called by God:

"And we know that in all things God works for the good of those who love Him, who have been called according to His purpose." Romans 8:28

"For those God foreknew, He also predestined to be conformed to the image of His Son, that He might be the firstborn among many brothers and sisters." Romans 8:29

"In the hope that I may somehow arouse my own people to envy and save some of them." Romans 11:14

"For God's gifts and His call are irrevocable." Romans 11:29

That evening, I went to the front of the church during the altar call and asked Jesus to forgive me of my sins (at that time my sins were along the lines of disobeying my parents, stealing candy from my sisters, fighting with my brothers, etc.). I loved Jesus then, and I do now— but I got lost along the way because I stopped fearing God and His precepts.

When I was nine, I wanted to follow Him and be used by Him however He saw fit. That night I prayed and found forgiveness, and I discovered my prayer language as well. I was baptized and filled with the Holy Spirit.

Covenant-Marriage Foundation

With building any structure, the foundation needs to be healthy and trustworthy. Your marriage, metaphorically, is a stout building— a castle.

You may say, "I already have a foundation for my marriage, and it's a great one," or, on the flip side, "My foundation is crumbling, and it's too late."

First of all, **it's never too late to build a healthy relationship with your spouse and get your marriage in line with God.** If the foundation to your home— or "castle" — is cracking, you first have to get it looked at and determine the issue. Next, you'll need to put the time and effort into it to get it fixed. Finally (and this is true whether it's already cracking or not), you have to upkeep it in order to reduce future damage.

What does a crack in the marriage foundation look like? They can reveal themselves in several ways, such as:

- Selfishness
- Lack of communication with spouse
- Anger
- Unforgiveness (leads to hardened heart and bitterness)
- Sexual immorality (emotional involvement is the first stage which can, and often does, lead to physical infidelity)
- Unbalanced and/or addictive behaviors (alcohol, drugs, food, gambling, and even personal hobbies)

- Financial carelessness

Sometimes cracks in the foundation are hard to see, and aren't noticed until it's too late. These cracks start out small, but they allow the enemy to slither into your marriage and set up outpost defenses, so they can make an orchestrated attack against your castle later. I'll share this Scripture with you a few times as you read this book:

"For our struggle is not against flesh and blood, but against the authorities, against the powers of this dark world, and against the spiritual forces of evil in the heavenly realms" Ephesians 6:12

This means people (your spouse, children, brothers, sisters, fathers, mothers, bosses, etc.) are not your enemy. Stephanie and I were nowhere near perfect when we looked in the mirror, and we saw a lot of the cracks I mentioned earlier. Consequently, the enemy slowly chiseled away at our spiritual foundation (and, ultimately, our marital castle).

But we were not each other's enemy— the devil was.

Stephanie and I married when we were both twenty years old. We met with the minister beforehand to talk about our vows. I recall him reading a statement about our promises, and he asked if we understood them. We both said yes, and I think we then signed an agreement of some sort confirming we understood. As I look back, I can see that I viewed marriage as more of a contract than a covenant. I understood that we were both in agreement to uphold our part of the marriage. **However, I didn't understand how God was the final cord in the bonding of our marriage agreement.** Once bound together with Him in agreement, He doesn't like it when the covenant is broken. I knew what God's word said about covenants, but I didn't realize how serious His position was on the subject. Stephanie, on the other hand, knew that when she married, she wanted it to be for life. Because her own parents got divorced when she was a child, she understood the pain that a divorce wreaks on the entire family, and she never wanted that pain for herself or her children. She understood the concept of covenant, but didn't realize that's what it was until our first *Married for Life* class.

I clearly remember the night we left our *Married for Life* class after discussing the power of covenant. We were in the car heading home— I was baffled that I looked at marriage as more of a contract between each spouse, and Stephanie was glad to finally understand what had always been in her heart.

What is a covenant to God? It's a promise between God and mankind. It's a relationship built around a substantial commitment, and it is binding. Covenant is mentioned 292 times in both the Old and New Testaments. There are numerous examples of a covenant between God and Man in His Word. Here are a few quick examples;

- God's covenant with Abraham (Genesis 17:4)
- God's covenant with Noah (Genesis 9)
- God's covenant with Moses (Exodus 5:22-6:12)
- God's covenant with Israel (Isaiah 43)
- God's covenant with David (2 Samuel 7:11-16, 1 Chronicles 17:11-14)
- God's New Covenant with you and I (Luke 22:20 and Hebrews 7:22)

In mentioning the above examples, we can begin to understand that God's covenant between man and woman, a one-flesh union, is serious business. Here's the point that really grabbed our attention:

God doesn't break covenant. He doesn't quit. He doesn't waiver. He's steadfast and never-changing.

When Stephanie and I made vows with each other in the presence of God, we entered a one-flesh, covenant relationship.

"That is why a man leaves his father and mother and is united to his wife, and they become one flesh." Genesis 2:24

Our "one-flesh" covenant is not only with each other, but it is in covenant with God. God's word is true, as it is written:

"All your words are true; all your righteous laws are eternal." Psalm 119:160

I believe the following verse says it best, and it is hugely important concerning covenant. Moses said to the heads of the tribes of Israel:

"This is what the Lord commands: When a man makes a vow to the Lord or takes an oath to obligate himself by a pledge, he must not break his word but must do everything he said." Numbers 30:1-2

Because we fear God, we obey Him. That is why, as believers, we must not break our covenants.

Today's society pushes us to believe when two people are married, they have a contract that binds them together, and if one party fails to keep their side of the contract (and, sometimes, even when they do) then divorce is the next option. I have even found marriage web sites that have **"Marriage is a Contract"** on their title pages.

Almost globally, some type of license is required to get married, and it's not unusual for couples to have a prenuptial agreement to determine where assets would be distributed, in the case of the seemingly-inevitable divorce. Have they failed before they even started?

Satan and his principalities, powers, and rulers, have worked hard to turn God's sacred relationship between man and woman into nothing more than a business transaction. Satan started this campaign to discredit God's marriage covenant as early as Adam and Eve in the Garden of Eden, and again when Moses was the leader of the Jewish people. Satan's process was to take a covenant between a man, woman, and God, and degrade the value and importance of the promise, making it nothing more than a business agreement.

He slowly chips away at the value of the marriage covenant; which God holds in high esteem. Why would Satan target marriage? The answer lies within the ancient Scriptures. In *Genesis 3,* Satan attempted to totally destroy the relationship of Adam and Eve by posing as a serpent and being "crafty" with Eve. Satan didn't want them to rely on God's wisdom and knowledge, so he enticed Eve to be selfish and have all knowledge herself so she could "be like God" (Genesis 3:5). One of his main strategies is to convince us to be selfish. He (deceivingly) promises that by being self-reliant, we no longer need to rely on anyone or— more importantly— God.

Later in the Bible, we read that the Pharisees tried to trap Jesus about divorce (Mark 10:2-9). Jesus asked them what Moses said concerning divorce, although He knew full well what they were going to say. The Pharisees replied that Moses allowed a man to give written notice of divorce to his wife and send her away. Nevertheless, in Mark 10:5, Jesus replied that Moses wrote the law because man's hearts were hardened against God. Jesus went on to say:

"'But at the beginning of creation God "made them male and female." "For this reason, a man will leave his father and mother and be united with his wife, and the two will become one flesh." Therefore, what God has joined together, let no one separate.'" Mark 10:6-9

No one was to separate or divorce, because marriage was an institution created by God to be a covenant relationship.

"So, God created mankind in his own image, in the image of God he created them; male and female he created them. God blessed them…" Genesis 1:27

Satan knows that a one-flesh marriage that is in line with God's teaching is blessed, powerful, and prevents the forces of darkness from causing havoc. This is the number one reason why Satan has vigorously attacked marriage since the beginning of time. His strategy is to tear the couple apart, because Satan knows that **a one-flesh marriage that is in a covenant relationship with God has the power to protect, to minister, to evangelize, and win souls for the kingdom of God.**

The covenant between one-flesh couples and God is the cornerstone of a marriage. I never looked at covenant as being the cornerstone of my marriage until the Holy Spirit pointed it out to me. Let me take this concept one step further: we know Jesus was called the Chief Cornerstone—rejected by man, but chosen by God. When a one-flesh marriage has Jesus as their cornerstone of faith, their foundation is engineered firmly and accurately from the start. A cornerstone is significant, as it is an immovable stone. It sets the direction for the entire structure. When I think of our faith in Jesus as the cornerstone of the marital foundation, I get excited, thinking of the fortress we are building (or, in our case, rebuilding).

"As you come to him, the Living Stone-rejected by humans but chosen by God and precious to him. You also like living stones, are being built into a spiritual house to be a holy priesthood, offering spiritual sacrifices acceptable to God through Jesus Christ. For in Scripture is says: 'See, I lay a stone in Zion, a chosen and precious cornerstone, and the one who trusts in him will never be put to shame.' Now to you who believe, this stone is precious. But to those who do not believe, 'The stone the builders rejected has become the cornerstone.'" 1 Peter 2:4-7

If Stephanie and I would've had a firm grasp on these concepts before we were married, or even shortly thereafter, our story would be profoundly different. Without God as the cornerstone of our covenant relationship, we quickly succumbed to worldly reasoning and the attacks of the enemy.

Chapter 6

Matters of the Heart

The Inner Keep

Historically, castles have been designed in many different fashions. The Normans were most responsible for establishing the castle architecture we know today, starting way back in the tenth century. Castles were homes intended to protect the Lord and Lady of the presiding land. As technology advanced, castles were upgraded to meet updated defense standards. The Keep (pronounced "Kype" in old English) was the fortified residences and towers where the royal family lived day in and day out. Some castles included an inner-keep. The inner-keep was a secret chamber, or room, where the royal family would retreat in case the Keep was compromised. If the castle was overrun, the inner-keep was a last resort for defenses (Morris, 2018).

Inner-keeps usually had walls four to eight feet thick, assembled from stones and concrete. Early-period concrete was made from volcanic ash and clay, which set a precedent for today's concrete. Entryways were designed with thick, large wooden doors that could be barred and blocked from the inside (Morris, 2018).

In cases of bombardments, or sieges, against the castle, the royal family would hold up in the keep or inner-keep until matters concluded. A tunnel hewn out deep under the castle, with a possible escape route, may have served as an inner-keep as well. As technology advanced, fortifications were erected with towers similar to the Tower of London— an architectural strategy found to be successful (Morris, 2018).

How does the inner-keep relate to our marriages? The Lord showed me that the inner-keep of a marital castle is where your heart, mind, and soul reside. The Scriptures give us warnings about guarding these precious, God-given jewels, because they are three elements that you need to keep intact in order to love God. Satan and his evil forces are eager to take out at least one of these critical elements, if not all of them. You must take proactive steps to protect these prized components of your body and one-flesh marriage, because Satan will target and attack them without end.

"Jesus Replied; 'Love the Lord your God with all your <u>heart</u> and with all your <u>soul</u> and with all your <u>mind</u>. This is the first and greatest commandment…'" Mathew 22:37-38

"Above all else, guard your <u>heart</u>, for everything you do flows from it." Proverbs 4:23

"You will keep in perfect peace those whose <u>minds</u> are steadfast, because they trust in you." Isaiah 26:3

"...The breastplate of righteousness in place [to protect your heart]." Ephesians 6:14

"Take the helmet of salvation [to protect your mind]." Ephesians 6:17

While praying one morning, the Holy Spirit took me by a vision to show me the inner keep. I was trying to figure out where I was, surrounded by walls and floors of stone, when His amazingly timely reply said, without a voice, "We're within the inner-castle. I want to show you the inner-keep, which is the heart of this structure." As I looked around, trying to quickly absorb and capture all I possibly could during the vision, it was further explained to me that the walls were several feet thick. I thought to myself, *that is a lot of stone.* He replied, "Generations upon generations have worked to build this structure." I was puzzled, because Stephanie and I had only been married for 34 years. I thought that I was possibly in another couple's marital castle from ancient of days. He spoke again, "Many ancestral generations have contributed to this marital castle."

To help me understand, I was transported to an open field, where I saw many generations appear, lined up single-file. It was obviously from both a groom's and bride's families, going from the present to ancient of days. The line of generations went down over the hill, winding across the fields and streams. The further the line went back, the color of the clothes changed. Most people wore black and had some type of hat on. I could not see the end of the generational lines— they were too long.

I then turned in the opposite direction and followed the bride's and groom's generational lines as they came to a point at the present, and together formed a large "V" on what appeared to be a large, flat rock (perfect for building a foundation on) that sat high on elevated ground.

I saw the bride's and groom's parents and family, as the vision was transformed into video, actively laying stone on the elevated ground, obviously working on the foundation of a future castle. I tried to focus to see their faces, but for some reason it wasn't allowed. I then saw the bride's two sets of grandparents and their families, and the groom's two sets of grandparents and their families, all working together to lay the stone that built the marital castle. Behind them, in single file, I saw four sets of great-great-grandparents, and families from both of the groom and bride's sides, increasing as it stretched further back the family line. This continued as far as the eye could see.

The Lord said, "All the generations you see, and those you can't, have contributed to building this marital castle." Then, in old silent film mode, I saw each person from the bride's and groom's lineage together at the large flat rock, laying down stone. Some laid large foundational stones, some cornerstones, while others created arches of stones. Everyone laid down at least one stone toward the building of this marital castle.

Back within the castle walls, I turned a tight corner and came to the end of the hallway. A very old wooden door, inlaid with armor, was just ahead. The door opened, and I could see it was very thick and reinforced from inside. Again, there was stone everywhere— on the floor, walls, and even above on the ceiling. I sensed the walls were thick here as well. The Lord then said, "This is your last fallback position in case you become overrun. Protect the matters of the heart from the enemy at all cost."

Repentance

Repentance is a matter of the heart. The Holy Spirit directed me to strategically write about repentance in this chapter because it's located in the inner-keep of your heart and soul. If you want to get your life and marriage on the right path, we need to level set expectations; you know the path that we must follow, the one that is narrow. Here's what God's Word says about repentance.

"For all have sinned and fall short of the glory of God." Romans 3:23

"Whoever conceals their sins does not prosper, but the one who confesses and renounces them finds mercy." Proverbs 28:13

"Repent then, and turn to God, so that your sins may be wiped out, that times of refreshing may come from the Lord." Act 3:19

"If you declare with your mouth, 'Jesus is Lord,' and believe in your heart that God raised him from the dead, you will be saved. For it is with your heart that you believe and are justified, and it is with your mouth that you profess your faith and are saved. As Scripture says, 'Anyone who believes in him will never be put to shame.'" Romans 10:9-11

God made the outdoors for us, and it is our playground in life. He commands us to take care of the earth and all the animals. Smelling the trees, flowers, and fresh air is what a lot of us live for, and I am no exception. I love it! When the weather is beautiful, most people want to be outside— sitting on the front porch, grilling in the back yard, or enjoying a park somewhere. I love to hike and be outdoors.

I was once hiking a trail in Eastern Kentucky, near Red River Gorge and Natural Bridge. The trail winds through and around rock formations, climbing about 1,000 feet. It is a beautiful hike with tremendous views.

I found myself at an intersection. If I turned left, the trail headed down the steep, rocky cliff and through large boulders. If I went straight, it's the path to the top of Natural Bridge, and it offers incredible views. However, there is a small sign warning all hikers that the straight path becomes narrow and could be impassable by some. To me, this sign was intriguing. I thought, *I want to see this narrow passage,* and asked myself, *Why can't I climb around it if it's too narrow?*

As I climbed, I learned that the dirt trail ends, and from there it is solid limestone. Before I knew it, I was up against a sheer cliff on my left and a 50 to 60-foot drop-off on my right. Then I approached the narrow gap, named Fat Man's Squeeze. Large-bodied hikers in front of me came to a screeching halt. Members in their party who were thin slipped right through the 30-foot-long narrow trail, and the others had to turn back. The large-bodied hikers were very disappointed. They had exerted so much energy to get to that elevation and point on the trail, and they didn't get to continue and see the final reward, the view. There was no way to climb up the face of the cliff or go below it. Due to this, they were routed back down the trail. Sometimes I've seen where if one hiker couldn't pass through the narrow passage, those that could would feel sorry for them and follow them back down the cliffs, never making it to the top. Amazingly, while on my hike and observing the situation the hikers were in, the Lord spoke to me and said, "This is very similar to the narrow path in My Word".

"But small is the gate and narrow the road that leads to life, and only a few find it." Mathew 7:14

The Holy Spirit conveyed that many want to walk through the gate or narrow path, but few will do it. The concept of repentance has been around since the beginning of time, don't be offended by His requirements for us to repent of our sins. It's possible you're not reading this book by accident. Have you thought that you may be the one that has wandered away from His flock, and this book is an attempt to reach out to you? This is how He does it. He will speak to you through Godly grandparents, parents, family members, managers, co-workers, friends, books (especially His Word), and even fortune cookies, believe it or not. What, you don't think God could send you a message in a fortune cookie? He spoke through a donkey (Numbers 22:28), and Christ said if we didn't praise Him, the rocks would cry out (Luke 19:40). In Isaiah, we see the mountains and hills burst out in song and the trees clap their hands.

"Then the LORD opened the donkey's mouth, and it said to Balaam, 'What have I done to you to make you beat me these three times?" Number 22:28

"'I tell you,' he replied, 'if they keep quiet, the stones will cry out.'" Luke 19:40

"You will go out in joy and be led forth in peace; the mountains and hills will burst into song before you, and all the trees of the field will clap their hands." Isaiah 55:12

Guard your thoughts, God can do anything He pleases, even if it is talking to you through a fortune cookie. If we truly want to get on the right path with God, we'll need to navigate repentance successfully. If we allow God into our space, He will give us insight and provide wise direction for our lives and marriages.

Please remember, this is an urgent message. We don't have a lot of time. I encourage you to take a chance on Him. Will you take some time, right now, to start fresh, start heading in the right direction, and level-set your life with Christ?

The following prayer is similar to what I prayed while sitting in my car in St. Petersburg, Florida. I had many wrongdoings over the years, especially when I selfishly left and moved to Florida. From your soul's inner keep, from the heart, say this prayer to reset your salvation for yourself, and your relationship with Jesus Christ.

"Dear Lord Jesus, thank you for dying on the cross for my sin. Please forgive me. Come into my life. I receive

You as my Lord and Savior. Now, help me to live for You the rest of this life. In the name of Jesus, I pray. Amen."

The original Greek word for repentance is "metanoia" (μετάνοια) which means to have "a transformative change of heart." In other words, to repent is to do an about-face and go in the opposite direction from where you were going.

It's important to mention that once you repent from your sins, you will need to start a personal, intimate, relationship with Jesus Christ, a relationship that leads to everlasting life.

I always knew what God's Word said about being in a relationship with Him, and I would have good intentions of starting on the narrow path... but before long, I would come to an intersection of temptation. I would take a detour off the narrow path, and never fully be committed to Christ. Essentially, when I repented, I turned away from my sin until it was inconvenient to myself— "self" being the key word.

My detours caused so much strife in my life and my marriage. Looking back, I was never securely on that narrow path. Although at times I was very close, I wasn't an overcomer. To be an overcomer, we have to fear God and obey His precepts, be disciplined against the temptations of our mind, the worldly desires of our flesh, and against what the evil dark forces may throw at us. Now, I'm fully committed to God. He has changed my life. Material things that I used to care about no longer hold me in chains. My main concern in life now is being obedient, and intimately ensuring that my life is in line with His word.

Another significant event that happened, once I returned home and repented at the altar with my wife, was water baptism. A couple of months later our church had a baptism service.

Once you repent from your sins, Jesus tells us that we should be baptized by submersion in water:

"Jesus replied, 'Very truly, I tell you, no one can see the kingdom of God unless they are <u>born again</u>.' 'How can someone be born when they are old?' Nicodemus asked. 'Surely they cannot enter a second time into their mother's womb to be born!' Jesus answered, 'Very truly I tell you, no one can enter the kingdom of God unless they are <u>born of water and the Spirit.</u> Flesh gives birth to flesh, but the Spirit gives birth to spirit. You should not be surprised at my saying, "You must be born again." The wind blows wherever it pleases. You hear its sound, but you cannot tell where it comes from or where it is going. So, it is with everyone born of the Spirit.'" John 3:3-8 (emphasis added)

Shortly after I accepted Christ when I was 9 years old, I was baptized and I said, "Here I am Lord." Since then, over the last 40 years, I had a couple of promptings from the Holy Spirit, asking me to be baptized as an adult. My pride shook it off, and I convinced myself that I didn't need to since I was baptized as a child. Hindsight tells me that there is a difference, especially if you fell away from Christ after having a relationship with Him, then rededicated your life. My pride also didn't want people to know that I had fallen away from God.

What is all the fuss about baptism? Well, the Greek word "baptizo" (βαπτιζω) implies immersion into water. To baptize is, "an act of immersion in water." The act of being baptized is identifying with Christ's death and burial. By emerging from the water, it signifies Christ's resurrection. We spiritually leave our old life and become a new creation.

Well, there I was, sitting in church, and our pastor announced, "Next weekend, we are having water baptisms." Pride spoke up, "You're good. You did this when you were a child. You don't want to get wet in front of a bunch of people, do you?" The Holy Spirit counteracted in a gentle, loving voice, "You need to do this." When I heard that, my whole being voted, "Yes!"

Have you ever had the experience of driving down the road, seeing a Dairy Queen, and asking the compliant little riders if anyone wants an ice cream cone? Happy yells, whoops, and cheers fill the car. This is how every part of me responded when He said, "You need to do this." My mind, body, heart, bones, and my soul were filled with an anxious anticipation. "Yes, Lord, I will do it." It was as if my flesh was cheering me on to be baptized. When your own flesh is cheering you on, how can you turn it down? Believe me, you don't want to turn down the Holy Spirit! Get baptized, and tell pride to check himself at the door.

By saying, "Yes Lord, I will be baptized," I was being obedient, and it was a public declaration of my faith, of my identifying with Christ.

My spirit knew I was free of sin because Jesus Christ forgave me, cleansed me, and washed me white as snow (Isaiah 1:18), making me 100% whole. My spirit didn't want any part of the sin, because it knew that to accept Christ and follow His guidelines meant life eternal. To not accept Christ essentially meant that I was dying at an accelerated rate. I was on the fast track to the grave.

The following week came, and I was baptized as my family stood by and watched. Tears flowed down my face again. Although it was cold getting out of the water into the chilled air, I felt 100% warm and in-line with Christ on the inside. It was a great feeling that I never want to give up again.

"Whoever believes and is baptized will be saved, but whoever does not believe will be condemned." Mark 16:16

"Those who live according to the flesh have their minds set on what the flesh desires; but those who live in accordance with the Spirit have their minds set on what the Spirit desires." Romans 8:5

"For if you live according to the flesh, you will die; but if by the Spirit you put to death the misdeeds of the body, you will live." Romans 8:13

Forgiveness

Just as Jesus has forgiven us for all our sins, we must also forgive. Forgiveness is another matter of the heart. God's Word commands us to forgive. In Matthew chapter 18, Peter asked Jesus about forgiveness.

"'Then Peter came to Him and said, "Lord, how often shall my brother sin against me, and I forgive him? Up to seven times?" Jesus said to him, "I do not say to you, up to seven times, but up to <u>seventy times seven</u>."' Matthew 18:21-22 (NKJV, emphasis added)

After hearing this command from Jesus, many will immediately start scanning their memory for the person or incident that offended them. I've rarely held onto an offense that someone committed against me personally. In situations where I was hurt, I typically forgave and moved on, even when I was embarrassed. *However*, when my children or wife were hurt in some way, I would get angry and hold on to that offense for a long time.

After our *Married for Life* small group discussed forgiveness, Stephanie and I both examined our lives. I personally had to look back into my childhood, to a very dark time, where I found unforgiveness still lurking in my heart.

I never told anyone that I was molested as a child. The first time I allowed myself to address the issue was when I was in my thirties. I never even exposed it to Stephanie until she and I were having marital problems and I agreed to speak with someone from our church. I was embarrassed, and I didn't want anyone to know. The counselor asked if I had ever been sexually abused, and my mind went into hyperdrive, but everything around me suddenly went into slow-motion, and I felt dizzy. I just looked at the counselor for what felt like forever, trying to determine if I should say anything. *Do I open the doors to my heart and expose my wounds and scars?* I was reluctant to answer.

As a side note, please be *very* careful who you "lower the drawbridge" for, allowing around your children or grandchildren. I was seven years old, safe and sound inside the walls of my parents' marital castle— or so they thought.

"The thief comes only to steal and kill and destroy; I have come that they may have life, and have it to the full." John 10:10

Because of this spiritual and physical attack on me as a child, I've always made it a personal agenda to take extra precautions in protecting children under my responsibility, be it family, extended family, or even children that have been in my care from church or community groups. It's hard to be vigilant all your life, especially if you're not taking precautions with God-given spiritual tools. Even with hyper vigilance, the enemy can still blindside us and enter in, in ways we never thought possible.

The week on forgiveness in our *Married for Life* small group resurrected all the past hurts and feelings of anger from when I was abused. I had to let it go. I forgave the person who sexually assaulted me, but it is something a seven-year-old boy should never have to go through. The damage was done. I was exposed to twisted, sexual perversions at the age of seven, and it would haunt me for years to come. Satan and his dark forces slithered into my parent's castle in the form of a family friend who was welcomed with open arms. He selected his prey and did the damage.

Over the years, when I heard people talking about pedophiles sexually assaulting children, I would have so much anger toward the offender. Satan's evil forces have no regard for your children and want— more than anything— to steal, kill, and destroy them. It was time to forgive my offender, and let Jesus start healing those wounds.

Forgiveness is ultimately not about the person who wronged us, but rather about our relationship with Christ. We are not letting that person off the hook, we are letting ourselves off the hook by saying "no" to disobedience, bitterness, and a hardened heart.

"For if you forgive other people when they sin against you, your heavenly Father will also forgive you. But if you do not forgive

*others their sins, your Father will not forgive your sins."
Mathew 6:14-15*

Without forgiveness, bitterness will fester and grow into hatred. If you have not forgiven the person who wronged you or your loved ones, bitterness will grow inside you and cause your heart to be hardened.

A hardened heart will move you further away from God.

Forgiving someone who has done evil against you is tough to do. Nevertheless, it is essential to getting your heart in the right place. I agree that the person who has wronged you should be the one to take the first step, but it's not worth the stress of worrying if, or when, that person will repent. It boils down to you being willing to forgive because God commands it.

I had to remember that the person who sexually assaulted me was not my enemy; the enemy was Satan and his evil forces.

God gives us an example in Hebrews 12:14-17, where He provides a warning, encouragement, and illustration on this matter of mistreating others: you will not be rewarded or forgiven. The Holy Spirit also reminded me of the Scripture which mentions that it will be harder to forgive in the last days (2 Timothy 3:3). So, not only is it against our nature because pride stands in the way, but the Scriptures tell us it will be even harder to forgive in the last days because hearts will grow cold. I believe we are in those days.

If you really want to reset your heart, improve your relationship with God, and build a better relationship with your spouse, *forgiveness is a must*— regardless of the offense. I've seen believers work hard to get their lives in line with Christ, but they have unforgiveness stored up in their hearts for someone who hurt them and they refuse to let it go. If you cannot forgive, you are allowing enemy strongholds to anchor in your heart.

In Luke 23:34, we read of Jesus saying, "Father, forgive them, for they do not know what they are doing." He said this while hanging on the cross, with people scoffing and soldiers gambled over His clothes.

Now, remember, Jesus was fully God yet also fully human. Take a step back and consider: if you were hanging on a cross with all that activity happening below you, it would be exceedingly hard to forgive those people. However, since He was human as we are, He set the example. Even in His worst hour, He was able to forgive. We are to do the same.

Take a moment here and speak this prayer out-loud: *"Heavenly Father, forgive me for those I have wronged. Help me to truly forgive those that have wronged me. I speak the person's name _____. I give all my wounds, hurts, and scars to You and ask that You mend my heart. Thank You, Lord! In Jesus Name, Amen."*

"...Because of the increase of wickedness, the love of most will grow cold..." Matthew 24:12

"Make every effort to live in peace with everyone and to be holy; without holiness no one will see the Lord. See to it that no one falls short of the grace of God and that no bitter root grows up to cause trouble and defile many. <u>See that no one is sexually immoral,</u> or is godless like Esau, who for a single meal sold his inheritance rights as the oldest son. Afterward, as you know, when he wanted to inherit this blessing, he was rejected. Even though he sought the blessing with tears, he could not change what he had done." Hebrews 12:14-17 (emphasis added)

Farming Your Relationships

Another important matter of the heart is sowing and reaping. As we all know, there are several kinds of natural laws that God created. An example of a well-known natural law is the law of gravity. Have you heard of the law of sowing and reaping? Did you know that the act of sowing and reaping is a matter of the heart?

I originally started to write "we have natural laws from the outcome of God creating the earth," but while writing that statement the Lord corrected me and said, "No, the laws don't exist because of cause and effect. I specifically created every natural law, and the details that surround them". I quickly resounded with, "Thank you, Lord, for providing insight and pointing that out to me."

I want to introduce you to my maternal grandfather Amnie. He was a coal miner until he retired at the age of 65. He and my grandmother, Caroline, rented 158 acres of farmland in southwestern Pennsylvania for approximately $35 a month, on a one-hundred-year lease. They had fourteen children, and, as you can imagine, numerous grandchildren and great-grandchildren.

When I was twelve years old, I was working on my farming merit badge for boy scouts, and as a result, I found myself spending the summer with my grandparents. My grandfather would plow the field, plant corn and wheat, and reap the harvest. He planted several apple trees, and ended up with an apple orchard producing many baskets of apples every year. He planted pear trees, and they provided pears. He planted grape vines and reaped the grape harvest annually. Lastly, he would feed the chickens and reap the benefits of eggs— and the occasional chicken dinner.

Although he only had a 2nd-grade education, my grandfather was a wise man. He understood the law of sowing and reaping, from both a farming and a family perspective. As a farmer, he understood the process of planting a seed, and the importance of five essential farming principals:

1. Planting
2. Watering
3. Cultivating
4. Fertilizing
5. Time

The process of planting seeds:
1. Plant the seed in fertile soil
2. Roots will need time to grow (depending on the planted seed, the roots from the seed may need additional *time* to grow deeper into the soil)
3. The seed will breach the soil and connect with sunlight as it transitions into a plant
4. The plant grows and leaves develop
5. The plant then produces fruit

Without one of the five farming principals, your harvest would be lacking potential harvest. The most impactful principal my grandfather understood was the *time* factor. He knew from experience that a planted seed needed time to grow and mature. When a plant started to produce leaves, he knew that it was on its way to producing fruit, but more time would be needed for the plant to go from producing leaves to bearing fruit. These are the farming fundamentals laid out since the beginning of time.

"As long as the earth endures, seedtime and harvest,
cold and heat, summer and winter, day and night
will never cease." Genesis 8:22

When the Holy Spirit brought my grandfather to my mind, He said, "When your grandfather sowed a *cup* of corn, I ensured that he reaped a *wagon load* of corn." Just as when a farmer sows a literal seed and expects to reap a harvest, we must expect to reap a harvest in the lives of those around us when we sow our metaphorical seeds.

What seeds are we talking about? They may be the things we say, our actions, our attitudes, or our motives. We can sow either positive or negative seeds in the lives of those around us.

Kind, encouraging words, pure motives, and a gentle attitude will reap a positive harvest.

Conversely, words and actions filled with anger or spite will bear a negative harvest. Have you ever gotten angry and spoken harshly with your child for breaking something? Did you see their little hearts become hurt, and their demeanor wither? You planted a negative seed. What if instead, you told them it was ok, helped them clean up the mess, and scooped them up in your arms for a hug? That positive seed would reap a positive harvest in your child.

The law of sowing and reaping may seem simple in the above example, but it really is just that simple. Sow positively, and you reap positively. Sow negative seed, and you will reap a negative harvest.

I encourage you to sow positive seeds into your relationships, especially those of your spouse and children. One small seed can yield a great return.

Here is another way of looking at sowing and reaping. Pay close attention to the first bullet below:

- Sow negative in; you get **greater** negative return
- Sow positive in; you get **greater** positive return
- Regardless of how you sow, it takes time to mature
- A key point to remember, **you always get more in return, whether positive or negative**

My grandfather's heart was kind, gentle, and loving. My grandmother was an amazing Sunday School Teacher and prayer warrior. They hosted a fantastic family reunion every year on the 4th of July. They understood that keeping family close was valuable, and bringing his many children, grandchildren, extended family, and friends together every year was one of his ways of sowing love and affection. My grandfather passed away in 1983 and now, 36 years later, the family still comes together on the 4th of July.

I was recently talking with several of my cousins, and I found that their visits to the farm are some of their best childhood memories. It was one of my fondest memories as well. The seed of love from my grandparents, planted into all of their family, has produced a harvest of amazing memories and love toward them, even years after they have been gone.

Have you ever taken a step back and wondered why your harvest wasn't what you were hoping for? For instance, I didn't feel like I was getting anywhere financially for many years. Looking back, it was because we stopped sowing into the church after we had been hurt at a particular church.

What you are reaping is a direct response to what you are sowing. Let me say that again—

You are reaping what you are sowing!

The law applies to all mankind, regardless, your opinion. Just because you may not think about this law doesn't mean you shouldn't apply the principle.

"Do not be deceived: God cannot be mocked. A man reaps what he sows. Whoever sows to please the flesh, from the flesh will reap destruction; whoever sows to please the Spirit, from the Spirit will reap eternal life." Galatians 6: 7-8

Another week, and Stephanie and I left our *Married for Life* small group truly examining what we were sowing into each other, our children, and our grandchildren. I wondered what I was sowing into my wife and marriage. I wanted positive returns from my wife, I wanted her to be happy, I wanted affectionate responses from her, and I wanted our relationship to grow and blossom.

To be honest, I wasn't always sowing positive comments or acts of love into my wife or family. My words weren't always encouraging, my attitude was in horrible shape, and sometimes my actions were even worse. It was time for a change in the right direction. Both Stephanie and I realized that God takes this subject very seriously, and now we consciously practice sowing positive seeds into each other— as well as our children, grandchildren, and others we come in contact with.

The Holy Spirit said, "Now look at your relationship with God. Are you sowing seeds of life or death?" I obeyed and started to think about my relationship with the Lord. To be honest, I sowed well in my younger years— but in the last ten years, I hadn't given much of myself, my time, or any of my earnings (tithe) to God. When I was giving, I felt like I was getting nowhere, and my heart had become bitter and hardened over the years. The Lord showed me that giving or sowing to God was a matter of the heart. Previously, I was giving because someone said I needed to. I wasn't giving to Him because I loved Him, I gave simply to obey. I've learned there is a significant difference.

Because I struggled with giving to God (through the church) after we had been hurt, the Holy Spirit spoke to me, lovingly and gently, about being generous, and about how giving God the first fruits of all my earnings would return many blessings to me. Giving God the first moments of my day, giving Him ten percent of my income, presenting Him with offerings, and blessing the less fortunate, were merely seeds that would yield a fantastic outcome. He pointed out to me that I wasn't giving to a preacher, or a church, or a building, but that I was giving to Him. It was my selfish heart that was refusing to give to the Lord.

He told me, "Although you may be sowing physically into a church, a pastor, or missionaries by giving literal dollars, in the spiritual realm, you're giving to Me— the God of the Universe, Creator of heaven and earth. Regardless of your opinion on how an establishment of Mine is managing the money you give; you should not concern yourself." He continued, "I don't need your money, I own it all. I multiply it and assign it. I correct and judge those that do not manage it efficiently. What pleases Me is when you want to give to Me without persuasion or reward. I want you to give from your heart that which is valuable to you, because you love Me." He reminded me that sowing in the Spirit is a matter of the heart— it gives life, not death. When giving to God the things I find valuable, I push those things aside and make Him number one in my life.

I remembered the Bible story from Sunday School of The Widow's Offering. She gave all that she had as an offering to the Lord. To give so much when you have nothing is truly giving from your heart.

I call this the paradox of giving. It's the opposite way from which many of us think. Our typical view is that we'll give to God when we have *extra* money, but He wants us to give Him our first fruits, even when we have little to offer. When we give from our hearts because we love God, it comes back to us abundantly.

"Jesus sat down opposite the place where the offerings were put and watched the crowd putting their money into the temple treasury. Many rich people threw in large amounts. But a poor widow came and put in two very small copper coins, worth only a few cents. Calling his disciples to him, Jesus said, 'Truly I tell you, this poor widow has put more into the treasury than all the others. They all gave out of their wealth; but she, out of her poverty, put in everything—all she had to live on.'" Mark 12:41-44

"Do not love the world or anything in the world. If anyone loves the world, love for the Father is not in them. For everything in the world-the lust of the flesh, the lust of the eyes, and the pride of life-comes not from the father but from the world. The world and its desires pass away, but whoever does the will of God lives forever." 1 John 2:15-17

I had been taught the principles of sowing and reaping all my life, starting in Sunday School, and portrayed in the excellent examples of my parents and grandparents. The light bulb regarding this principle had come on when I returned from Florida and reconciled with Stephanie, but now it was getting much brighter. I was seeing the status of my heart more clearly now. It was time to turn my focus on God, and get my giving status back in check. It was time to give from my heart because I love and adore Him.

"Give, and it will be given to you. A good measure, pressed down, shaken together and running over, will be poured into your lap. For with the measure you use, it will be measured to you." Luke 6:38

Chapter 7

The Castellum Keep

The Latin word "castellum" originally meant "Roman fortlet" or "tower". The keep was usually the first structure built, a round tower where jewels, precious valuables, and perhaps even legal documents, could be stored in safety. It would serve as the initial fortress, while other related structures were built to enhance the keep and maintain safety. The keep was the heart of the castle. During attacks or sieges, it housed the most beloved people of the royal family, such as the queen, princesses, and princes. The king, in most cases, would be found elsewhere, directing the battle. The keep had the most comfortable living rooms, bedrooms, kitchens, and dining areas within the castellum. (Morris, 2018)

One particular morning, I had my alarm clock set for 4 AM because I wanted to be ready and waiting for the Holy Spirit when He visited me. I noticed the more I praised Him before I went to bed, the stronger I felt His presence. It was almost a sure thing that He would visit around the 4th watch.

Stephanie was traveling with her mom on a two-week vacation. In the early morning, I heard my phone go off. I was barely conscious and ignored it, falling back into a sound sleep. I have my text notification set to a tweeting bird, so the notification sound is not alarming, but gives me a friendly, gentle alert when I receive a text message. That particular morning, I heard it tweet two or three more times in rapid succession, as if I had text messages pouring in. I thought that maybe Stephanie was trying to get my attention... perhaps there was a problem. I finally reached for my phone, and I realized, to my surprise, that I had no text messages. I wondered what had just happened. I looked at the time, it was 2:55 AM. Then I knew... it must be the Holy Spirit trying to get my attention.

I immediately started to pray and turned on some worship music, then the visions started again. I found myself floating in the main entrance of the castle, just inside the large, arched wooden doors. It appeared to be a large foyer, with a massive double-staircase ascending upward from the middle of the entrance. The foyer was created with beautiful stones. I could see large paintings hanging on the walls, but I couldn't make out the faces or images on the paintings.

I sensed a celestial and benevolent spirit beside me, which I assumed was the Holy Spirit. I wanted to turn and face Him, but an understanding came over me that looking at Him was not allowed. We ascended the stairs as if we were flying, which was a great way to travel through that magnificent fortress. Looking down at the foyer, I noticed that the walls were lined, about ten feet tall, with beautiful oak wood. The staircase was white marble, and the hand railings and rungs were made of white-painted wood. Waiting for us, at the top of the stairs, was a large room with a red carpet. We glided up to a large wooden door, with an arched trim over it. I sensed that the door was in place for security reasons.

We passed through the door without it ever opening. Without needing to ask, I knew we were in the keep of the castle. I saw a rich library of books from all over the world, with an adjacent sitting room. Farther down the hall, bedrooms lined both sides of a large hallway. There were canopy beds, couches, and fantastic art on the walls.

I was able to focus on one of the large paintings. He asked, "Do you know what place the painting portrays"? I looked at the picture and instinctively knew that it was the Garden of Eden. It was so beautiful— with magnificent shade trees, fruit trees, and various animals casually going about their day. The painting depicted a place of tranquility, showing the splendor of the garden. On another wall was a large portrait of a man and woman, just married. I saw the groom and the bride dressed in white, with a crowd of people celebrating. The couple was riding in a carriage pulled by white horses.

As the vision continued to develop, I saw myself walking up a flight of stairs. Each step on the staircase revealed more details regarding the different rooms of the castle, and their marriage-related subcategories. The Holy Spirit pointed out that honesty, trust, and physical intimacy were all key components that dwelt within the keep of the marital castle. These components are essential to a healthy marriage.

The Holy Spirit said, "Finalize this chapter with how Jesus loves the church and the church loves Me, which is the ultimate example for all men to follow in loving their wives, and for women to follow in loving their husbands." (Ephesians 5:22-33)

Honesty

As you can imagine, this is an area I failed in before leaving my wife and family in 2016. I knew the right direction to go, but inadvertently chose to ignore it. I thought I was in good standing with God, when in fact I was lost. It caused a lot of grave, hurtful damage in my relationship with my wife and children. The scars I created will be there for years to come. Nevertheless, praise be to God, we have seen what should have been deep, lasting scars, being healed in an escalated manner.

I'm sure you know that honesty and respect are paramount to developing a stable relationship with your spouse. It is elementary and fundamental to a marriage, but sometimes we need to be reminded of the basics in order to stay on the right path.

Unfortunately, many people find it easier to tell a "little white lie" about an issue than to address it head-first. Lies aren't always meant to hurt your spouse, but they will rapidly degrade trust— and, ultimately, your relationship.

Let's take an authentic look at the real enemy, the father of all lies (John 8:44). I think there is value in looking at the spiritual side of honesty, since dishonesty is against what our Creator commanded.

"The Lord detests lying lips, but he delights in people who are trustworthy." Proverbs 12:22

Keep in mind that Satan's first recorded lie is written in Genesis 3:1. Satan, dwelling within the serpent, told Eve that she would certainly *not* die if she ate the fruit from the Tree of Knowledge of Good and Evil (in exact contradiction to what the Lord had said). Subsequently, the lie perpetuated and caught Adam in Satan's web of lies, too. Satan is the father of all lies, which means that lies originated from him, and it is one of his primary weapons against us.

"During a conversation with other Jews, Jesus said: 'You belong to your father, the devil, and you want to carry out your father's desires. He [Satan] was a murderer from the beginning, not holding to the truth, for there is no truth in him. When he lies, he speaks his native language, for he is a liar and the father of all lies.'" John 8:44

Satan's native language is lies, and this weapon of his is successful when people believe him.

The size of the lie doesn't matter.

Little white lies are the same as big, elaborate lies. Adolf Hitler, a man obviously used by the evil one to spread abhorrent lies, once said, "If you tell a big enough lie, and tell it frequently enough, it will be believed." (*Mein Kampf*, Adolf Hitler, White Wolf, 2014)

Satan has lied to angels and to Jesus Christ Himself, so there's no stopping him using lies in his tactics against husband and wife.

The truth is, God has commanded us to not bear false witness against one another.

"You shall not give false testimony against your neighbor." Exodus 20:16

"Do not lie to each other, since you have taken off your old self with its practices." Colossians 3:9

Now that we know the fundamentals of honesty, we can use it to our advantage in our marriages and relationships. Imagine using honesty as an advantage…think about the possibilities of building a stable relationship, founded on an honest character.

"Dear Children, let us not love with words or speech but with actions and in truth." 1 John 3:18

When the truth is used as a foundational cornerstone, it builds a trustworthy character, which is one of the best character traits a person can cultivate in a marriage or relationship.

Trust

Trust is another area we are working on rebuilding within our marriage. Using honesty as a foundational building block, I intend to restore trust within our marriage and never break it again. I knew I couldn't do it by myself, and neither could Stephanie. She would be crazy to unconditionally trust me, considering what I had done in the past. It is only through the guidance of the Holy Spirit, and our trust in God, that we can take the steps to earn (me) and give (Stephanie) trust. With God all things are possible.

"Jesus looked at them and said, 'With man, this is impossible, but with God all things are possible.'" Matthew 19:26

Jesus is all about forgiveness, reconciliation, and redemption. If you think you are unworthy to receive any of these for you or your marriage, think again. Even if you have been divorced, the Lord will forgive you.

"The LORD is merciful and gracious, Slow to anger, and abounding in mercy." Psalm 103:8 (NKJV)

It is essential that you act and speak in ways that build trust. Be truthful in not only what you do, but also your motives and thought patterns. Tell your spouse you love him/her, and do it often. Complimenting another person sows positive seeds into the relationship. Keep in mind, one negative comment needs almost twenty positive comments to balance out the one negative seed. As a rule of thumb, make a point never to deliver negative remarks to your spouse, since it builds walls of distrust, and separates you and your spouse even further.

"The hearts of the wise make their mouths prudent, and their lips promote instruction. Gracious words are a honeycomb, sweet to the soul and healing to the bones." Proverbs 16:23-24

"Words from the mouth of the wise are gracious, but fools are consumed by their own lips." Ecclesiastes 10:12

Separation and selfishness are precisely where Satan wants to take you. The Lord showed me in Genesis 3:1 that Satan tempted Eve to think about herself, and move her from relying on God into a self-relying status. After Satan tempted Eve, telling her to eat of the fruit of the tree of the knowledge of good and evil, he said that she would become like God and surely would not die.

Through Satan's tempting, Eve had a desire to be wise like God, and she disobeyed His command by eating of the fruit. When this happened, there was a transformation in her heart, away from God. When we only think about ourselves and personal gain, it's like we're the walking dead, Satan's hands on each of our shoulders, steering us farther away from Christ.

"Then the serpent said to the woman, 'You will not surely die. For God knows that in the day you eat of it your eyes will be opened, and you will be like God, knowing good and evil.'" Genesis 3:4-5 (NKJV)

Stephanie and I found that the less we think about the desires of our own hearts, and concentrate instead on serving each other, the closer our relationship moves toward God.

Honor your spouse by sharing your schedules, your accounts, and your passwords. Sharing passwords really makes an honesty statement. It helps to remove doubt, and it builds trust. It also adds a layer of accountability to your relationship. 1 Corinthians 13:5 is a prime example of how to love and respect your spouse:

"[Love] does not dishonor others, it is not self-seeking; it is not easily angered; it keeps no record of wrongs..." 1 Corinthians 13:5

I know we're all busy. If you and your spouse are anything like us, it seems like there is no end to our activities and responsibilities. It's easy, as life speeds by, to miss out on truly connecting with your spouse when they speak. I admit there are times when I miss everything my wife tells me, simply because my mind was not present. Often, she'll say, "I just told you that, but you weren't listening." Occasionally she misses what I say, but not often.

I heard a saying once, regarding conversations with other people, that goes, "Be here, now." When speaking with your spouse, take the time to sincerely listen to what they have to say. Listen with your eyes and heart. Provide responses that confirm that you are listening.

Take time to focus on your spouse when they're talking to you, and press the pause button frequently. Remember, treat them with respect, because their opinion matters on everything that happens in your marriage and family. Your spouse has concerns, fears, and frustrations, and they need to know you can be trusted with them. By listening intently to your spouse, and giving them your undivided attention, you will see trust deepen in your relationship.

Other actions to think about that will assist in building trust with your spouse.

- Keep secrets between the two of you **secret.**
- Work when at work, and not when at home.
    - When at home, be focused on your spouse and family, you must draw the line.
    - If you work from home, identify a particular cutoff time and stick to it. By not doing this the message you convey is, "family is not important".

- - The enemy wants to disrupt your family life, don't give into it. God will reward you for making a stand.
- Take time to laugh together, and learn how to find smiles.
  - *Proverbs 5:18*
- Your word must be paramount. Don't go back on it.
  - *Proverbs 25:19*
- When you fail, admit it.
  - *Proverbs 14:16*
  - *Ephesians 4:31-32*
- Transparency is a must.
  - To start, consider opening a joint email account.
  - Make it easy for your spouse to trust you by allowing them to know your actions.
  - Share locations using your phone.
  - We need to go out of our way to ensure that trust is being soundly practiced.
  - *2 Corinthians 8:21*
- Always try to work and be together as a one-flesh couple whenever possible.
  - Stephanie and I started a new practice of serving *together* at church. It's essential to not separate, because this could open the door for the enemy to enter into your relationship and separate you.
  - *Mark 10:8*

We've found that honesty and trust bind our relationship together and make us stronger as one.

"The man said, 'This is now bone of my bones and flesh of my flesh; she shall be called "woman," for she was taken out of man.' That is why a man leaves his father and mother and is united to his wife, and they become one flesh. Adam and his wife were both naked, and they felt no shame." Genesis 23:24-25

Physical Intimacy

As Stephanie and I dug into the week of physical intimacy in our *Married for Life* class, the coaches pointed toward the covenant between our one-flesh relationship and how God was the designer of the intimacy between a man and a woman. That was a fun week in our class, in more ways than one, because we got to watch other couples' reactions to the way God created physical intimacy to be done in His one-flesh marriages.

Our homework that week was to go home and practice physical intimacy the way God intends.

The *Married for Life* book points out that, "You can tell how important something is to the true heart of God by how much time the enemy spends perverting it" (Phillipps, 2012). The scriptures make it clear that the enemy has been working to pervert the physical intimacy found in the biblical marriage union since the beginning of time. As I mentioned previously, Satan's first attack on marriage can be found in Genesis 3. Because of the way man has twisted God's Word, the Holy Spirit emphasized that I was to write the following:

A marriage is a sacred institution between a man and a woman.

Relationships between man and man, or woman and woman, are detestable to God.

He loves all men and women because they are His children. Nevertheless, those that disregard His Word or twist it to fit their choices are making the willful decision to sin against Him.

Satan has persuaded men and women to accept bogus physical intimacy that has distorted God's original intention for the marriage bed. These include homosexuality, fornication, adultery, incest, and self-satisfying sexual acts, in the form of masturbation.

"Do not have sexual relations with a man as one does with a woman; that is detestable." Leviticus 18:22

"But a man who commits adultery has no sense; whoever does so destroy himself. Blows and disgrace are his lot, and his shame will never be wiped away." Proverbs 6:32-33

"Flee from sexual immorality. All other sins a person commits are outside the body, but whoever sins sexually, sins against their own body." 1 Corinthians 6:18

Unfortunately, Satan has completely perverted marital sex, and most marriages may never really experience physical intimacy the way God intended it. Typically, when a marriage is outside of God's one-flesh model, one of the spouses is out to satisfy their own lustful desires. When this happens, their heart becomes hard, and this leads to lustful sex versus God-ordained sex (sexual intimacy with love and tenderness). Men and women continually seek a better way of fulfillment, but never achieve it. Subsequently, the other spouse can feel rejected, used, or unsatisfied during intimacy. The way women tend to view themselves often reveals insecurity or a lack of self-image. This feeling can spread like burning wildfire into other parts of the marriage.

It's important to know that there are profound, hostile effects of sexual sin on one's mind, heart, and soul. God's design for sexual intimacy is pure and rewarding. Why did God create sex? It wasn't intended for individuals, but instead to be experienced in a marriage union. He created it to be something that generates awesome pleasure and emotional satisfaction for a man and woman *together*, and— as an important secondary role— to procreate the earth.

"Do nothing out of selfish ambition or vain conceit. Rather, in humility value others above yourselves, not looking to your own interests but each of you to the interests of the others." Philippians 2:3-4

We know, through scripture, that a man and woman have a body (sexual), soul (friendship), and spirit (spirituality through the Holy Spirit) when in a one-flesh marriage.

"May God himself, the God of peace, sanctify you through and through. May your whole spirit, soul, and body be kept blameless at the coming of our Lord Jesus Christ." 1 Thessalonians 5:23

"For the word of God is alive and active. Sharper than any double-edged sword, it penetrates even to dividing soul and spirit, joints and marrow; it judges the thoughts and attitudes of the heart." Hebrews 4:12

Want to take your physical intimacy to the next level? Developing the three components of body, soul, and spirit will escalate your one-flesh physical intimacy relationship.

How to develop Body, Soul, and Spirit:
1. **Body**: Take walks together, workout together, keep your personal hygiene in check.
2. **Soul**: Spend time hanging out together, talk with each other, dig into deep, friendly conversations. When was the last time you asked your spouse's opinion and heard them out?
3. **Spirit**: Read God's word, pray, seek spiritual intimacy (obedience, repentance, forgiveness, honesty, trust, and sowing).

Take some time to read the Song of Solomon. In it, God reveals, in lovely language, the intimate relationship between a man and a woman. In the Song of Solomon, we learn that sexual arousal comes from hearing your spouse's voice and enjoying them intimately, physically up close to you. As you read through it, pay attention to the contrast between the way God's Word describes physical intimacy between a man and woman, and the way Satan and his dark forces have perverted sexual relationships through a multitude of media.

God shows His sexual plan to us through His Word, if only we take the time to read it. God's plan for physical intimacy is gentle, selfless, and caring. In the example of Ezekiel 16:8, see how God, the groom, treats his wife, the Children of Israel.

"Later I passed by, and when I looked at you and saw that you were old enough for love, I spread the corner of my garment over you and covered your naked body. I gave you my solemn oath and entered into a covenant with you,' declares the Sovereign LORD, 'and you became mine.'" Ezekiel 16:8

If you have experienced sexual sin, God always gives us an out. You simply have to repent (which we already discussed in chapter five).

"Husbands, in the same way, be considerate as you live with your wives, and treat them with respect as the weaker partner

and as heirs with you of the gracious gift of life, so that nothing will hinder your prayers." 1 Peter 3:7

"Now for the matters you wrote about: 'It is good for a man not to have sexual relations with a woman.' But since sexual immorality is occurring, each man should have sexual relations with his own wife, and each woman with her own husband. The husband should fulfill his marital duty to his wife, and likewise the wife to her husband. The wife does not have authority over her own body but yields it to her husband. In the same way, the husband does not have authority over his own body but yields it to his wife. Do not deprive each other except perhaps by mutual consent and for a time, so that you may devote yourselves to prayer. Then come together again so that Satan will not tempt you because of your lack of self-control." 1 Corinthians 7:1-5

Stephanie and I have been attending the Vow conference at our church since we reconciled in late 2017. The Vow conference is a time for married couples to come together as one-flesh for good food, fellowship, and to hear guest speakers on different perspectives of developing and improving marriage. Looking back, it is interesting that we didn't attend the Vow conference in 2016. Neither of us had any interest, which should have been a red flag that we were in trouble. Moving forward, we'll never miss it.

In 2018, Dr. Gary Chapman was a guest speaker during the conference, speaking about his book *The Five*

Love Languages. Stephanie and I read the book before the conference so we could be well informed when Dr. Chapman shared his view on the topic. I found it so refreshing to better understand my wife's love languages, and how understanding them could improve our physical intimacy with each other. That information helped me to know how to respond to her, and her to me.

    I found that Stephanie was more responsive to me when I was spending quality time with her. God made women to be sensitive to a man, to respond to different aspects of her husband's love for her. Creating a time and place for us to spend quality time together showed her that I cared, and it would eventually lead to more intimacy between us. It's vital that we put self in the back seat, especially where physical intimacy is concerned.

Check out Dr. Chapman's book, *The Five Love Languages*, here: www.5lovelanguages.com

    What are some ways to improve your physical intimacy? Spruce it up with the suggestions listed here:
1. Read God's Word, and Bible-based literature, on physical intimacy.
2. Sit down with each other and discuss your sex life. Have a two-way conversation.
3. Schedule frequent times when you can both get physical.
4. Be creative, and have fun when getting physical.

5. Pray about your physical intimacy time.
6. Pray together before times of intimacy (this is a really good suggestion).
7. Flirt with each other during the day, or throughout your week.

Love~The way Jesus Loves His Church

Love is the last component found within the castellum keep. It completes the foundations and fundamentals needed for the keep of your marriage. When repentance, forgiveness, sowing, honesty, trust, and God's plan for physical intimacy are practiced, it allows God's love to surround the man and woman in ways not many marriages experience.

I believe this is one of the main reasons why the Lord wants these principles emphasized; so that marriages everywhere can be reconciled to the love of our Heavenly Father. These principles are from the Bible, and have been around since the beginning of time. It never passes away, but Satan wants to subdue God's Word so you cannot know Him personally.

"Heaven and earth will pass away, but my words will never pass away." Matthew 24:35

As Stephanie and I continued through the *Married for Life* course, I found my love for her grew to a new level of unconditional love. I had always loved her, but now found my passion for her growing. I had greater respect for her. Without a doubt, the Lord cultivated the small seed of love in my heart for my wife, just as her heart is growing for me.

I love my wife more now than I ever have in my 34 years of marriage. It is not at the level we once had; it is a completely new level of love that I've never experienced. This new love has everything to do with getting my personal relationship with God in the right place. It's surely a God thing, taking a small seed and growing it into something magnificent.

While in the early stages of writing this book, the Holy Spirit had been speaking to me about this section, and I'm excited to discuss the example that Jesus gives to us on how He loves His bride, and the bride loves Him.

We don't need to look at a Merriam-Webster dictionary for the definition of "love," since God has defined it well in His Word. In fact, many of us have heard what He has to say about love, found in 1 Corinthians 13:

"Love is patient, love is kind. It does not envy, it does not boast, it is not proud. It does not dishonor others, it is not self-seeking, it is not easily angered, it keeps no record of wrongs. Love does not delight in evil but rejoices with the truth. It always protects, always trusts, always hopes, always perseveres. Love never fails..." 1 Corinthians 13:4-8

God's Word has been instilled in my heart since I was a small child, but during the times when I wasn't wholeheartedly serving the Lord, my soul cringed when I heard scripture. It was offensive to me.

However, once my relationship with Jesus grew deeper, I noticed that His Word abides in me like never before. Now, when I hear His Word, it is refreshing to my soul.

I love that so many will turn to 1 Corinthians 13 for the definition of love, but it's sad that they reject everything else in the Bible because they do not consider it relevant for today (or maybe their free will is in conflict with His Word).

God's love for us is never-ending, and we will never be separated from it. *If only each of us could love our spouse the same way God loves us.* He is modeling the love we should adopt for our spouses. In Romans chapter eight, He tells how deep His love is for us.

"Who shall separate us from the love of Christ? Shall trouble or hardship or persecution or famine or nakedness or danger or sword? As it is written: 'For your sake, we face death all day long; we are considered as sheep to be slaughtered.' No, in all these things we are more than conquerors through him who loved us. For I am convinced that neither death nor life, neither angels nor demons, neither the present nor the future, nor any powers, neither height nor depth, nor anything else in all creation, will be able to separate us from the love of God that is in Christ Jesus our Lord." Romans 8:35-39

"Follow God's example, therefore, as dearly loved children and walk in the way of love, just as Christ loved us and gave himself up for us as a fragrant offering and sacrifice to God." Ephesians 5:1-2

One Flesh: This is a Profound Mystery

"For this reason, a man will leave his father and mother and be united to his wife, and the two will become one flesh. <u>This is a profound mystery</u>..." Ephesians 5:31-32 (emphasis added)

Most people love a good mystery, so let's investigate the biblical secret of the one-flesh union together.

When God creates anything, He is very precise about the details. This mystery is one example of how God, the Chief Architect, designed the striking parallel between *Jesus and the church*, and *the marriage union between a man and woman*. Marriage is a mystery; it conceals a definition that is much deeper than what we see at the surface. Jesus is the head, and the church is the body. As Jesus and the church become one, so are the husband and the wife to become one flesh.

The mystery continues when a man and woman marry; they are supernaturally tied together by their souls, and this is where we get the term "soul ties." The husband is the head, and the wife is the heart.

As a side note, it is significant to point out that "soul ties" can happen between anyone: unmarried men and women, friendships, and even people you work with on a daily basis. Soul tie connections happen spiritually, through physical or emotional relationships. Often, we're not aware of the effect these soul ties have on us spiritually.

There are two types of "soul ties": godly and ungodly.

Godly soul ties are those relationships that abide within the parameters of God's word.

Ungodly soul ties occur when the thoughts and actions of those around us have an influence on us spiritually.

A great example of an ungodly soul tie is perhaps a teenage first love where an emotional and/or physical relationship developed. Another example may be where a dear friend has confided in you and has confessed sin.

As we move forward to emulate Christ, it's important that we break the ungodly bindings and influences, and prayer is an incredibly effective way of cutting those ties. "Lord, I pray that You cut all ungodly soul ties that I have with (**name of person**). Amen" (1 Samuel 18:1; Proverbs 1:10,15; 1 Corinthians 6:16).

Another significant mystery is that the roles of the husband and wife are not irrationally assigned. The roots are firm within the unique roles of Christ and His bride, the church. What I find amazing is that Paul, when writing Ephesians, was shown the mystery of Christ and the church as a foundation for God's pattern for love in marriages. The husband and wife should make every effort to model their marriages after this perfect, pure design found in Christ and the church.

Shiddukhin: A Mutual Covenant

It is essential to understand the Hebrew marriage process, since John 3:29 portrays Jesus as the bridegroom of the church, and the church as His bride.

In the books of John and Revelation, we see that there is a parallel between the way Jesus loves the church, and how the husband is commanded to love his wife. The ancient Hebrew wedding ceremony is beautiful, and it tells the story of love. The detail of the steps taken shows how much love and care were placed in the process. There are three different steps to a Hebrew wedding.

1. shiddukhin (mutual covenant),
2. erusin (betrothal)
3. nissuin (marriage).

"The Lord God said, 'It is not good for the man to be alone. I will make a helper suitable for him.'" Genesis 2:18

The preliminary process before a legal betrothal is called *Shiddukhin* in Hebrew (Johnson, 1903). The bride was often selected by the father of the groom, as was the case where Abraham chose Isaac's bride.

"Abraham was now very old, and the LORD had blessed him in every way. He said to the senior servant in his household,

the one in charge of all that he had, 'Put your hand under my thigh. I want you to swear by the LORD, the God of heaven and the God of earth that you will not get a wife for my son from the daughters of the Canaanites, among whom I am living, but will go to my country and my own relatives and get a wife for my son Isaac.'" Genesis 24:1-4

In ancient days, marriage was more practical and often served as an alliance for survival. Romantic love wasn't really necessary, and often was not considered, although there was always the hope that romance would eventually grow. When the alliance was created for the parents' selfish ambitions or glory, instead of the well-being of the couple and glory of God, I believe that it was a perversion of God's original, intended plan. Once again, man perverted God's will to work for his purposes.

Days before the betrothal, both the bride and groom were prepared for the ceremony by being separately immersed in water, in a Hebrew ritual called mikvah. This represents a spiritual cleansing by water submersion. Scripture tells us that John baptized Jesus in the waters at the Jordan River.

"Then Jesus came from Galilee to the Jordan to be baptized by John. But John tried to deter him, saying, 'I need to be baptized by you, and do you come to me?' Jesus replied, 'Let it be so now; it is proper for us to do this to fulfill all righteousness.' Then John consented. As soon as Jesus was baptized, he went up out

of the water. At that moment, heaven was opened, and he saw the Spirit of God descending like a dove and alighting on him. And a voice from heaven said, 'This is my Son, whom I love; with him, I am well pleased.'" Matthew 3:13-17

Likewise, you and I are the church, and as the bride-to-be we are also asked to be immersed in water.

"Whoever believes and is baptized will be saved, but whoever does not believe will be condemned." Mark 16:16

Erusin: The Betrothal

"He who finds a wife finds what is good and receives favor from the Lord." Proverbs 18:22

After the couple is baptized, they enter into a marriage canopy, called the *huppah*, where they hold a public ceremony surrounded by family and friends. The huppah canopy is symbolic of a new household being established with a binding covenant.

While in the marriage canopy, the groom provides a gift to the bride, usually consisting of money or a valuable object, such as a ring. The couple's covenant vows are then sealed by sharing a cup of the most excellent wine. The couple then enters into the betrothal period. This typically lasted about a year. Although they were considered married, they did not live together or engage in sexual relations during the betrothal period.

As a point of interest, it was during the betrothal period that the angel came to Mary to inform her of her pregnancy with Jesus (Matthew 1:18).

The *Erusin* period is when the groom was away, prepping and building a place for his bride. (Johnson, 1903)

Meanwhile, the bride was focusing on her personal preparations, such as her wedding dress, garments, and lamps. Keep in mind there were no telegrams, phone calls, or text messaging going on between the groom and bride. It was possible that the couple did not see each other for an entire year.

The bride would expect her groom to return for her in approximately a year, but she did not know the exact day or hour he would return.

The groom's father mentored him through the wedding process. He provided the money to pay the bride's ransom to her parents, he gave the groom guidance, and he gave him approval to return to claim his bride.

The betrothal period was a time when the couple's hearts were full of excitement and anticipation of one day being together. During that time, the bride kept her oil lamps filled because the bridegroom could return any time, even during the night.

As the groom and bride would depart to return to their prepared home, the wedding procession would sound the *shofar*, a ram's horn, in celebration of the event. Jesus used the Hebrew wedding process, (in the example of Ten Virgins) to illustrate the exclusive period of *Erusin*, and His own future return to snatch away His church.

"At that time, the kingdom of heaven will be like ten virgins who took their lamps and went out to meet the bridegroom. Five of them were foolish, and five were wise. The foolish ones took their lamps but did not take any oil with them. The wise ones, however, took oil in jars along with their lamps. The bridegroom was a long time in coming,

and they all became drowsy and fell asleep. At midnight, the cry rang out: 'Here's the bridegroom! Come out to meet him!' Then all the virgins woke up and trimmed their lamps. The foolish ones said to the wise, 'Give us some of your oil; our lamps are going out.' No,' they replied, 'there may not be enough for both us and you. Instead, go to those who sell oil and buy some for yourselves.' But while they were on their way to buy the oil, the bridegroom arrived. The virgins who were ready went in with him to the wedding banquet. And the door was shut. Later, the others also came. 'Lord, Lord,' they said, 'open the door for us!' But he replied, 'Truly I tell you; I don't know you.' Therefore, keep watch, because you do not know the day or the hour." Matthew 25: 1-13

Jesus warns us to keep our relationship with Him intimate by ensuring that the oil within our hearts never runs out. Making Him the most important focus in all you do will safeguard you for when Christ returns.

Nissuin: The Marriage

"And if I go and prepare a place for you, I will come back and take you to be with me that you also may be where I am." John 14:3

In the ancient Hebrew wedding, the final step was to take the bride away. *Naso* is a Hebrew root word meaning to lift up, and *Nissuin* in Hebrew means to take (*Naso nissuin*= lift up and take).

On the day Stephanie and I were married, my mother and sisters sternly warned me that I was not to see my bride before the ceremony. Traditionally, it is discouraged for most Christian grooms to see their bride until the musician plays the bridal entrance song. In our day, the favorite was "Here Comes the Bride". Slowly, the bride entered and walked toward the front of the church. That is precisely how it happened for me. My heart leaped, and I thought, *Wow!! Look how beautiful she is! I'm the luckiest guy in the world*!

Even though I knew it was Stephanie, it wasn't until she was standing beside me, and the veil was removed, that I confirmed the fact that Stephanie was the woman in the wedding dress. It may seem strange to say that, but the next story addresses the point I'm trying to make.

In Genesis 29:18-30, we read that Jacob loved Rachel so dearly that he agreed to work for Laban, her father, for seven years in order to marry her. After the seven years ended, Laban deceived Jacob by secretly replacing Rachel with her older sister, Leah, under the veil. Jacob eventually gave another seven years to Laban for Rachel, the love of his life.

The deception that Laban committed against Jacob has shaped the Jewish wedding ceremony from ancient times to present. Today, the Jewish custom is that the groom *must* see the bride before the ceremony.

Soon after the wedding ceremony, the groom carries home his bride with much celebration. Once home, the groom and bride consummate their marriage and live as a one-flesh couple, fulfilling the covenant of marriage (Johnson, 1903).

"Husbands, love your wives, just as Christ loved the church and gave himself up for her to make her holy, cleansing her by the washing with water through the word, and to present her to himself as a radiant church, without stain or wrinkle or any other blemish, but holy and blameless. In this same way, husbands ought to love their wives as their own bodies. He who loves his wife loves himself. After all, no one ever hated their own body, but they feed and care for their body, just as Christ does the church." Ephesians 5:25-29

Husbands, serve your wives as Christ serves the church. Cherish her as a gem given to you as a gift from God. Communicate your love for her. Confirm your love for her by serving her, touching her with gentle hands, buying her gifts, and spending quality time with her.

What is your view of your spouse? Is it positive or negative? I challenge you to take a chance with God, follow His guidance, change your view of your spouse, and start looking at them as if looking through God's eyes. Love them exclusively, start speaking their love language, and make every effort to show your love for them. If God can change my heart and make it bubble over with love for my wife, He can do it for you and your spouse.

"Be devoted to one another in love. Honor one another above yourselves." Romans 12:10

"However, each one of you also must love his wife as he loves himself, and the wife must respect her husband." Ephesians 5:33

When will the marriage of Christ and the Church take place? After Christ comes for the church, His bride, at the rapture. Imagine the magnificence and grandeur of a wedding in paradise!

I know the events surrounding the return of Christ can be confusing. I briefly explain the rapture of the church and the second coming of Christ in the next section, *The Marriage Supper of the Lamb*.

The Marriage Supper of the Lamb

Since we've been talking about the holy marriage between Christ and His church, the Holy Spirit nudged me to go ahead and mention The Marriage Supper of the Lamb. He reminded me that there is someone who hasn't heard this yet, and He wants to bless them.

"Blessed is the one who reads aloud the words of this prophecy, and blessed are those who hear it and take to heart what is written in it because the time is near." Revelation 1:3

As we saw earlier, since ancient days up until the present, the husband returns to take his bride. The bride anxiously awaits that special day. She falls asleep at night, dreaming of her new life with him. She asks questions like, *what will life be like in our new home? What will it be like in the land of my new husband?* Her heart is overwhelmed with hope, joy, and the start of their relationship under the same roof. Excitement is in the air as she enthusiastically looks out the window, and down the road, for his grand return.

The Bible tells us that Jesus (the Bridegroom, John 3:29), has gone before us to prepare a place for us, His bride (the church). Jesus, who is the Messiah of all men and women, will soon return to lift up, and take away, His waiting bride into the heavens.

The Bible also tells us that, just like in ancient times, a bride price (or ransom) was paid for Christ's bride. Jesus paid that bride price for you and for me when He died on the cross. Unfortunately, there are many who think this is just a metaphor, or some fantasy made up by man. I agree it sounds dreamlike, but that is what faith is all about, believing in that which is unseen (Hebrews 11:1).

"Do not let your hearts be troubled. You believe in God; believe also in me. My Father's house has many rooms; if that were not so, would I have told you that I am going there to prepare a place for you? And if I go and prepare a place for you, I will come back and take you to be with me that you also may be where I am. You know the way to the place where I am going." John 14:2-4

"Do you not know that your bodies are temples of the Holy Spirit, who is in you, whom you have received from God? You are not your own; you were bought at a price. Therefore, honor God with your bodies." 1 Corinthians 6:19-20

If you have accepted Christ as your savior and repented of your sins, then you are the bride of Christ. As the bride, you must do everything in your power to keep the lamp burning bright within you in preparation for the Bridegroom's return, just as in the parable of the Ten Virgins (Matthew 25). The Lord has been pressing this concept into my spirit, so that I should tell everyone.

The really good news is that Christ is coming back for His bride, and it will happen in the twinkling of an eye. The believers will be caught-up and transitioned to resurrected bodies instantaneously. This is yet another mystery, because the dead will be raised, imperishable and changed. This was an unheard-of idea to the apostles, and was never prophesied by Old Testament prophets or writers.

It's imperative to mention that Christ's coming in the last days is in two parts. Many misunderstand the scriptures which are meant to explain His rapture of the church and His second coming. I've outlined them in the next two distinct sections, "The Blessed Hope" and "Second Coming."

The Blessed Hope:

The Blessed Hope is what Paul calls this highly anticipated event— what many believers call the <u>Rapture</u>. An event like no other ever experienced on earth, because of the magnitude of the impact.

*"While we wait for **the blessed hope**—the appearing of the glory of our great God and Savior, Jesus Christ..." Titus 2:13 (emphasis added)*

God's Word tells us that this "taking away" has happened five other times in the history of man, and two remain (#6 and #7 below).
1. Enoch (Gen. 5:21-24)
2. Moses (Deut. 34:5-8)
3. Elijah (2 Ki. 2:11-14)
4. Jesus Resurrection/Rapture (1 Cor. 15:20-24)
5. Old Testament Saints (Matt. 27:51-53)
6. Rapture of the Church (1 Thes. 5:2-4)
7. Two Witnesses (Rev. 11:4-6)

One important note about the Rapture is that only God knows the day, hour, and moment when it will happen. Neither Jesus, the Holy Spirit, nor the angels in heaven know when this imminent event will occur. Scripture tells us that all the dead in Christ shall rise and meet Jesus in the air.

A broad consensus of those who know and understand this mystery of the rapture believe that Jesus will snatch up 50% of the earth's population. They base their assumption off of the parable of the Ten Virgins (Matthew 25:1-13)- five were taken by the groom, and five were not. However, I believe the raptured church may be more like 10%-20% of the population. Remember, it's a narrow path, and not many will pass through the gate. I also believe that this is why the Holy Spirit has been pressing me, around the clock, to get this urgent message on the street. He wants to take as many of His believers with Him who, like the five virgins, are watching with the flames bright within their heart. In order to be like the five good virgins, you must have an intimate relationship with Christ.

One of the last warnings the apostle Peter gives us in scripture is about scoffers. Scoffers will mock the return of Christ. They will say, "Where is this coming He promised?"

The Merriam-Webster dictionary defines scoffing as "an expression of scorn, derision, or contempt." Those who scoff at the return of Christ are sure to be left behind when He comes. One essential thought we must keep in mind is that a thousand years is like a day to God, and a day is like a thousand years. What has been thousands of years to us, since Peter wrote those words, has only been a matter of days to God.

A Thousand Years are like a Day to God
But do not forget this one thing, dear friends: With the Lord a day is like a thousand years, and a thousand years are like a day. 2 Peter 3:8

The Day or Hour Unknown
"But about that day or hour no one knows, not even the angels in heaven, nor the Son, but only the Father. As it was in the days of Noah, so it will be at the coming of the Son of Man. For in the days before the flood, people were eating and drinking, marrying and giving in marriage, up to the day Noah entered the ark; and they knew nothing about what would happen until the flood came and took them all away. That is how it will be at the coming of the Son of Man. Two men will be in the field; one will be taken, and the one left. Two women will be grinding with a hand mill; one will be taken, and the other left." Matthew 24:36-41

Jesus' Coming is Imminent!
"Be patient, then, brothers and sisters, until the Lord's coming. See how the farmer waits for the land to yield its valuable crop, patiently waiting for the autumn and spring rains. You too, be patient and stand firm, because the Lord's coming is near. Don't grumble against one another, brothers and sisters, or you will be judged. The Judge is standing at the door!" James 5:7-9

Archangel's Voice will be Heard

"For the Lord, himself will come down from heaven, with a loud command, with the voice of the archangel and with the trumpet call of God, and the dead in Christ will rise first. After that, we who are still alive and are left will be caught up together with them in the clouds to meet the Lord in the air. And so, we will be with the Lord forever." 1 Thessalonians 4:16-17

"We know that the whole creation has been groaning as in the pains of childbirth right up to the present time. Not only so, but we ourselves, who have the first fruits of the Spirit, groan inwardly as we wait eagerly for our adoption to sonship, the redemption of our bodies." Romans 8:22-23

"Listen, I tell you a mystery: We will not all sleep, but we will all be changed—in a flash, in the twinkling of an eye, at the last trumpet. For the trumpet will sound, the dead will be raised imperishable, and we will be changed. For the perishable must clothe itself with the imperishable, and the mortal with immortality. When the perishable has been clothed with the imperishable and the mortal with immortality, then the saying that is written will come true: 'Death has been swallowed up in victory.'

'Where, O death, is your victory?
Where, O death, is your sting?'

The sting of death is sin, and the power of sin is the law. But thanks be to God! He gives us the victory through our Lord

Jesus Christ. Therefore, my dear brothers and sisters, stand firm. Let nothing move you. Always give yourselves fully to the work of the Lord, because you know that your labor in the Lord is not in vain." 1 Corinthians 15:51-58

"But our citizenship is in heaven. And we eagerly await a Savior from there, the Lord Jesus Christ, who, by the power that enables him to bring everything under his control, will transform our lowly bodies so that they will be like his glorious body." Philippians 3:20-21

"Brothers and sisters, we do not want you to be uninformed about those who sleep in death, so that you do not grieve like the rest of mankind, who have no hope." 1 Thessalonians 4:13

"Dear friends, now we are children of God, and what we will be has not yet been made known. But we know that when Christ appears, we shall be like him, for we shall see him as he is. All who have this hope in him purify themselves, just as he is pure." 1 John 3:2-3

Second Coming:

The second coming of Christ is more brilliant! It's after the second coming that the Marriage Supper of the Lamb will take place. There are similarities, as well as distinctions, in the two returns of Christ. I look at the rapture of the church as a soft extraction of the saints. Jesus will gently raise the dead from sleeping, and snatch away His living church.

The second coming is more of a battle charge, with King Jesus leading. We learn in the book of Acts (1:9-11) that Jesus will appear in a visible, physical body, and that He will be glorified. We also know that all inhabitants of the earth will see the second coming. Revelation tells us that all who see Him coming will wail and mourn. Jesus will be returning as the King of kings and Lord of lords, with blazing, fiery red eyes and riding a white horse. He will be coming through the clouds of heaven with power and glory.

I believe that the absolute awe of this image will put those who denied Him into a state of fear. Their hearts will become very heavy. They will probably realize the biggest mistake of their lives, and they'll feel used and deceived by Satan. The Bible tells us that all enemies of Christ will be instantly defeated. After the final battle is won, Jesus will ascend to the Mount of Olives, where He will pass judgement on the nations, and on those who did not accept Him as their Lord and Savior. Then the Marriage Supper of the Lamb will take place. It will be the capstone to the second coming of Christ.

"...This will happen when the Lord Jesus is revealed from heaven in blazing fire with his powerful angels." 2 Thessalonians 1:7

"*After he said this, he was taken up before their very eyes, and a cloud hid him from their sight. They were looking intently up into the sky as he was going, when suddenly two men dressed in white stood beside them. 'Men of Galilee,' they said, 'why do you stand here looking into the sky? This same Jesus, who has been taken from you into heaven, will come back in the same way you have seen him go into heaven.'"* Acts 1:9-11

But the Lord is Patient with You

"Above all, you must understand that in the last days scoffers will come, scoffing and following their own evil desires. They will say, 'Where is this "coming" he promised? Ever since our ancestors died, everything goes on as it has since the beginning of creation.' But they deliberately forget that long ago by God's word the heavens came into being and the earth was formed out of water and by water. By these waters also the world of that time was deluged and destroyed. By the same word, the present heavens and earth are reserved for fire, being kept for the day of judgment and destruction of the ungodly. But do not forget this one thing, dear friends: With

the Lord a day is like a thousand years, and a thousand years are like a day. <u>*The Lord is not slow in keeping his promise, as some understand slowness. Instead He is patient with you, not wanting anyone to perish, but everyone to come to repentance.*</u>

But the day of the Lord will come like a thief. The heavens will disappear with a roar; the elements will be destroyed by fire, and the earth and everything done in it will be laid bare. Since everything will be destroyed in this way, what kind of people ought you to be? You ought to live holy and godly lives as you look forward to the day of God and speed its coming. That day will bring about the destruction of the heavens by fire, and the elements will melt in the heat. But in keeping with his promise, we are looking forward to a new heaven and a new earth, where righteousness dwells.

So then, dear friends, since you are looking forward to this, make every effort to be found spotless, blameless and at peace with him. Bear in mind that our Lord's patience means salvation, just as our dear brother Paul also wrote you with the wisdom that God gave him. He writes the same way in all his letters, speaking in them of these matters. His letters contain some things that are hard to understand, which ignorant and unstable people distort, as they do the other Scriptures, to their own destruction. Therefore, <u>*dear friends, since you have been forewarned, be on your guard so that you may not be carried away by the error of the lawless and fall*</u>

<u>*from your secure position.*</u> *But grow in the grace and knowledge of our Lord and Savior Jesus Christ. To him be glory both now and forever! Amen."* 2 Peter 3:3-18 (emphasis added)

Whose Rider is Called Faithful and True

"I saw heaven standing open and there before me was a white horse, whose rider is called Faithful and True. With justice, he judges and wages war. His eyes are like blazing fire, and on his head are many crowns. He has a name written on him that no one knows but he himself. He is dressed in a robe dipped in blood, and his name is the Word of God. The armies of heaven were following him, riding on white horses and dressed in fine linen, white and clean. Coming out of his mouth is a sharp sword with which to strike down the nations. 'He will rule them with an iron scepter.' He treads the winepress of the fury of the wrath of God Almighty. On his robe and on his thigh, he has this name written:

KING OF KINGS AND LORD OF LORDS."
Revelation 19:11-16

" Then I saw 'a new heaven and a new earth,' for the first heaven and the first earth had passed away, and there was no longer any sea. I saw the Holy City, the new Jerusalem, coming down out of heaven from God, prepared as a bride beautifully dressed for her husband." Revelation 21:1-2

"Look, I am coming soon! My reward is with me, and I will give to each person according to what they have done. ... The Spirit and the bride say, 'Come!' And let the one who hears say, 'Come!' Let the one who is thirsty come; and let the one who wishes take the free gift of the water of life." Revelation 22:12, 17

Chapter 8

The Great Dining Hall

"Come with me," the Holy Spirit invited, "I want to show you more of this marital castle."

Up to this point, I had only seen the Inner-Keep and the Keep, so I was excited to see more. He took me up a stone staircase that spiraled upward in a clockwise direction. I automatically knew it was a secret passage, a shortcut to wherever He was taking me. The staircase was made of beautifully hewn stones, interlaced with black and white marble.

After ascending a couple of floors, I was brought into an enormous, open hall. The hall had a long wooden table, lined with chairs, in the center of the room. The table was long enough to fit 30-50 people—large enough for the immediate and extended family of the one-flesh marriage. Natural light from the windows brightened the room and flickered off the hickory wood floors.

The ceilings were approximately twenty feet in height. I was amazed at what I saw painted on the ceiling—hand-painted figures of all kinds, grouped in stories of the family, and painted in beautiful colors. I saw farms, pastures, people, dogs, angels doing warfare against snakes, and what appeared to be a family crest with military insignias. Near the many windows were comfortable, reclining chairs and smaller, round wooden tables. I imagined the occupants of the castle lounging in the chairs and taking in the beautiful views while enjoying their day, perhaps before or after a meal.

Three of the walls were filled with tall, rectangular glass windows. Between the windows hung beautiful drapes with embroidered stories from the Bible. On one of the drapes I saw the story of God feeding manna to the Jewish people while they wandered in the desert. On another drape, I saw the story of Jesus feeding the multitude of 5,000 with only five loaves of bread and two fish. Lastly, I saw a picture of the apostles sitting with Jesus in the upper room at the last supper.

I was drawn to the windows, where I looked out to see the view. My eyes were filled with the beauty of the sights and vivid colors of the landscape. I inhaled with big eyes. The views were so stunning, and I could see the landscape with perfect vision. The castle sat on high ground, which put my location in the hall at least sixty to one hundred feet above the castle's guarded entrances below.

This being my first view of the outside, I could clearly see how this marital castle was strategically built for security and keeping the enemy at bay. I looked and saw beautiful green fields, and blue lakes in the distance. I was at least one thousand feet above the distant fields and lakes.

In the far distance were the silhouettes of white-capped mountains, with beautiful white streams flowing into the lakes. I could see trees blowing gently in the wind, and the crops in the fields were waving, as if they were trying to get my attention. I leaned forward and focused, trying to get a better look at the crops to confirm what I was seeing.

The Holy Spirit helped me zoom in with high definition clarity, as if I had imaginary binoculars. The crops were praising the God of heaven with their dancing, by waving their stems and leaves. I was speechless. I thought, *if the crops are praising the Lord, then what should I be doing*? He turned my attention to the trees, and as they gently swayed they, too, came alive. A chorus of different sounds, that I would not normally have heard, was brought to my attention. I heard bees buzzing a heavenly song, backed up by a chorus of insects and birds. I listened to the low bass sound of the water falling from high places, which joined in with the trees blowing in the wind. It was orchestrated, cheering and very loud, as one might hear at a professional sports arena. They all cheered and praised God.

It was clear to me, from my viewpoint, that all the created things of the earth sang out and praised God without ceasing. I knew this is why the mountains, lakes, rivers, oceans, trees, crops, animals, and even humans were created— to be in a relationship with Him and give Him glory. They would praise, then rest, and then start again. They did this over and over throughout their assigned tenures.

He said, "You are now in the great dining hall of the marital castle. Jesus is the bread of life, and His blood is the drink of life." He instructed me to explain John 6:53-58, concerning the bread of life, before I started the chapter about the Armory, because He showed me that no soldier can go into battle without proper nourishment. I was confused at first, because I thought the topic of "Christ as the Bread of Life" didn't fit very well just before the armory chapter.

However, it slowly became clear why we were starting in the great dining hall of this beautiful fortress. I started to think about my Army days, and how John 6:53-58 ties in with the next chapter of armor, weapons, and tactics.

In our world, all Army, Air Force, Navy, Marines, and Coast Guard installations have several dining facilities (DFAC), chow halls, or galleys where service men and women go to nourish their bodies. DFACs serve breakfast, lunch, and dinner. Have you heard the old cliché, "You are what you eat?" In the next several paragraphs you will get a better understanding of how what you are eating, both spiritually and physically, could provide nourishment for your body or be working against you, to ultimately kill you.

For once, I leaned not on my understanding and just kept typing. I started to see the paradigm of The Bread of Life as I dug into it a bit. I realized that spiritual warriors prayed three times a day, just as military members eat three times a day. The Bible has amazing examples of those who prayed frequently.

King David confessed in Psalm 55:17 that he cries out to God three times a day; morning, noon, and night. Daniel prayed three times a day, even knowing that the penalty was death (Daniel 6:10). Most importantly, Jesus gave us the ultimate example of a prayer life. Not only did He pray three times a day, He prayed without ceasing. In my research, I found sixty-nine examples in scripture of Jesus praying to the Father. He prayed in the early morning, He prayed at the temple while teaching, and He prayed in the evening. These examples were just a fraction of His prayer life.

"Very early in the morning, while it was still dark, Jesus got up, left the house and went off to a solitary place, where he prayed." Mark 1:35

"Evening, morning, and noon, I cry out in distress, and he hears my voice." Psalm 55:17

"Now when Daniel learned that the decree had been published, he went home to his upstairs room where the windows opened toward Jerusalem. Three times a day, he got down on his knees and prayed, giving thanks to his God, just as he had done before." Daniel 6:10

"...while I was still in prayer, Gabriel, the man I had seen in the earlier vision, came to me in swift flight about the time of the evening sacrifice." Daniel 9:21

"But seek first his kingdom and his righteousness, and all these things will be given to you as well." Matthew 6:33

John 6:53-58 has very deep meaning, although reading the passage at face value can confuse many, just as it did Jesus' disciples. When He spoke of, "eating the flesh of the Son of Man and drinking His blood," they thought He was talking of cannibalism. Many of His followers departed from Jesus after He spoke about the bread of life, because they lacked understanding. With Jesus' crucifixion and resurrection behind us, along with supporting scriptures from the apostles, we can now draw conclusions, understanding, knowledge, and wisdom from the passage.

"For in him, all things were created: things in heaven and on earth, visible and invisible, whether thrones or powers or rulers or authorities; all things have been created through him and for him." Colossians 1:16

"Trust in the LORD with all your heart and lean not on your own understanding." Proverbs 3:5

"Jesus said to them, 'Very truly I tell you, unless you eat the flesh of the Son of Man and drink his blood, you have no life in you. Whoever eats my flesh and drinks my blood has eternal life, and I will raise them up at the last day. For my flesh is real food and my blood is real drink. Whoever eats my flesh and drinks my blood remains in me, and I in them. Just as the living Father sent me and I live because of the Father, so the one who feeds on me will live because of me. This is the bread that came

down from heaven. Your ancestors ate manna and died, but whoever feeds on this bread will live forever.'" John 6:53-58

"On hearing it, many of his disciples said, 'This is a hard teaching. Who can accept it?'" John 6:60

John 6:53-58
The Bread of Life Explained

Jesus calls himself the "Son of Man" because, in the days of Jesus, there was no New Testament. He was the living, breathing version of the New Testament. The scrolls of the Old Testament were truth, and were the only scriptures the people had. The Old Testament prophets and writers mentioned the Messiah as the "Son of Man," which expresses the Lord's human nature.

The "flesh" and "blood" are distinctively separate from one another, and tie back to the humanity of Christ. We know Christ had a faultless human nature as His identity. This was crucial, in order for Him to be a sacrifice for our sins.

Eating Christ's flesh and drinking His blood is symbolic. As believers, we understand that Christ has come as God incarnate (which means, "embodied in flesh"), that He was, at once, truly man and truly God. His flesh was a gift to mankind, and His blood was shed for our sins. By partaking in the symbolic flesh and blood of Christ, we enjoy several unimplied gifts (such as grace and redemption) obtained by His sacrifice. We are offered peace and validation in who we are in Christ. As we feed on Him, who is the living Word of God, we gain knowledge, wisdom, and relationship. Through Jesus' flesh and blood, we can sustain and preserve spiritual life.

Jesus tells us that without Him, a person has no righteousness and can do nothing of eternal significance (John 15:15, Matthew 6:33). Without feeding on Christ's flesh and blood, a person feeds on their own fleshly/sinful desires, which leads to eternal death. Let me emphasize that *there is no in-between.*

What we learn in John 6:53-58 is that we have to be in a committed relationship with God and his Son, Jesus, in order to gain access to— and use— spiritual weapons. Once I thought about it for a while, it made sense.

The Holy Spirit was showing me that spiritual warriors need to be well nourished in the spirit, or they won't last long on the battlefield. Here lies yet another paradigm where the physical and spiritual worlds travel in parallel: Jesus is our spiritual food and drink; our spirits absolutely need Him for battle. Without Him, we fail. The more we pray, worship, praise, and soak in His Word, the closer we get to Him, and the stronger He becomes in our lives.

"In the beginning, was the Word, and the Word was with God, and the Word was God. He was with God in the beginning. Through him, all things were made; without him, nothing was made that has been made. In him was life, and that life was the light of all mankind. The light shines in the darkness, and the darkness has not overcome it." John 1:1-5

"And without faith, it is impossible to please God because anyone who comes to him must believe that he exists and that he rewards those who earnestly seek him."
Hebrew 11:6

Chapter 9

The Marital Armory

If you had a choice, what would your "job" be in heaven? Would it mirror something similar to what you do now? We know that worshipping and serving the Lord will be paramount while in heaven, and the scriptures tell us that we will never grow weak or tired in serving God. Can you imagine having full-throttle energy that never runs out? I get excited just thinking about it.

When I consider this topic of heavenly "jobs", there is one thought that continues to force its way to the top of my consciousness; I'm confident if I were in heaven, I would be a warrior for the Lord. Of course, God is going to be the One who ultimately decides what we do in heaven, but don't you imagine that your job in heaven will be something you enjoy? I served in the Army and enjoyed the adventure, anticipation, and strategy of being on the battlefield, be it during peace or wartime. Likewise, my spirit gets excited when I think of being a warrior in God's army.

Recently, Stephanie and I joined forces with another couple to pray and lay hands on a brother in Christ. As we started to pray in the spirit, I stepped into a captivating vision. The Holy Spirit "transferred" the brother and me to a battlefield in a desert location, with mountains all around. The Lord was showing me that my brother in Christ was, indeed, a warrior in His army. He asked me, "Do you know where you are"? Although I have been in many desert locations, I did not recognize the place in the vision. Nevertheless, I somehow knew where I was. I replied with a question, "Armageddon?" He said, "Yes!"

In the spiritual realm, just on the other side of the veil between this world and the spirit world, we were standing on the hot desert floor with dust in our faces, kicked up by the traffic of people and machines. I looked around and saw we were on the front battle lines, amongst a vast army of those who are sanctified in Christ. None other than King Jesus was the commander.

We were at least 100 meters down the line to His right. The vision was better than 1080p high definition, and extremely realistic, going into great detail. There were many warriors dressed for battle. I looked across the desert floor and saw the enemy— the dragon and ancient serpent, Satan, and his demon army. The vision pointed toward a coming event that my brother in Christ and I would be part of. I was thrilled to think that Jesus would consider me worthy enough to serve in His army. God created men to be protectors. Since we are made in God's image, this shows us that He is a warrior as well.

"So, God created mankind in his own image, in the image of God he created them; male and female he created them." Genesis 1:27

"The great dragon was hurled down—that ancient serpent called the devil, or Satan, who leads the whole world astray. He was hurled to the earth, and his angels with him." Revelation 12:9

Stephanie and I were in our tenth week of *Married for Life*, and as soon as we sat down to discuss Spiritual Warfare, the vision started again. I heard what the coaches were saying, but it was challenging to focus. The Holy Spirit took me back to the marital castle, into the castle's armory. This time, the vision of the castle was different. He took me through the great halls and corridors, showing me the different rooms as we went deeper into the marital castle. We finally arrived at the Armory. He articulated, through more images and visions, the components of the armory and how I would express them here.

The armory is the place where spiritual weapons are stored. It's also where plans, strategies, and tactics for spiritual warfare, are kept under lock and key— incredibly well guarded. I said, "Lord, this is more like a war-room!" He replied, "They are linked, but I want to point out specific armor and weapons that are available to My one-flesh marriages for fighting their flesh, the world, and the evil one. We'll discuss the war room later."

As the Holy Spirit took me on a tour of the armory, and pointed out all the spiritual armor and weapons available to us as believers, I was amazed at what I saw, and the way He organized it.

Spiritual Gifts, Armor, Weapons, and Enemy

Armor of God

During the fourth watch, between 3-6 am, the Holy Spirit woke me. Waking in the early morning was happening more frequently, and I was exhausted during the day. I lay there, barely conscious, asking the Lord if I could have a few more minutes to sleep. Still lying on my back, I started to pray, but my prayers quickly turned to mumbling. I probably didn't say much before I was fast asleep again.

I felt the palm of a hand gently touch and push on the center of my chest, just over my heart. My eyes popped wide open. I looked over at Stephanie, because she can be a prankster at times and I thought she'd been the one who pushed on my chest— but she was deeply asleep. I looked around the room, but I didn't see anyone. Was I just touched by an angel? I sat up in shock. I'll admit, I was a little concerned and fearful. I was thinking, *what just happened*?

The Holy Spirit said, in His calming, peaceful voice, "Come and pray, spend time with Me." I immediately obeyed, and went directly to my private prayer place. Keeping pace with the Holy Spirit is extremely tiring.

Nevertheless, the time is so sweet. I wouldn't trade it for the world.

The Holy Spirit kept telling me that this book was urgent, and I was to be sure to meet the timeline He laid before me. I thought back to the New Testament and realized that Jesus' pace was relentless. He was always about His Father's business.

While writing this book, there have been mornings that I slept through the fourth watch. When I wake at 7 am, and realize that I missed worship and prayer during the fourth watch, I'll admit that I've thought the Holy Spirit must have had more pressing matters. I felt left out.

I decided that I didn't want to wait for Him to wake me anymore, but I wanted to be up and ready, waiting on Him. I began to set my alarm for the fourth watch in order to pray, worship, study the Bible, and listen for His voice.

During one particular fourth watch, the Holy Spirit showed me more about the Armor of God. I stepped into a clear vision, and I could tell we were below the main floor of the castle, walking through a stone corridor. We made a slight right turn through a doorway into the armory. It appeared to be a transition room, where a soldier would only pass through long enough to adorn his armor and select weapons. I immediately noticed that the armor was positioned on the left, and the weapons were attached to the wall on the right. The armory was reinforced with shiny metal. I was subconsciously told that this metal was stronger than steel-alloy, or any metal found on earth. No human could access the armory except by the Holy Spirit.

The room was clean, organized, and well maintained. The weapons were all made of fantastic quality, and carefully placed on a particular mounting device. I could see that all the spiritual weapons were well-cared-for and clean. The armor and weapons appeared to be standard weapons like you might see in medieval times, but I knew they represented spiritual weapons.

Both the armor and weapons were fitted according to the specifications of each person in the marital castle; husband, wife, and the children still living within the castle. I noticed beautiful gems lining the outside of the shields and the handles of the swords. I could tell they were of great value because of the way they sparkled, and also because of the uncanny gift of understanding while in the spiritual realm.

I thought it strange that the gems were on the outside of the shield, and wondered how they were not destroyed in battle. The Holy Spirit explained, without words, that the gems represented the spiritual gifts of the owner of the armor.

It was revealed to me that once a warrior comes into the armory, they adorn their armor of God in a specific order, then they select their weapons for the battle. He then explained the order in which a warrior puts on his armor: first he puts on the belt of truth, then straps on the breastplate of righteousness, covers his feet in the gospel of peace, grasps the shield of faith, and adorns the helmet of salvation. Lastly, he takes hold of the sword of the spirit. The warrior will then be watchful with the eyes of his heart, with prayer always on his lips.

The Holy Spirit showed me armor that had never been used, and some that was only lightly used. He said, "Some armor is never adorned, and therefore is never used."

I assumed the following:

1. The person whom the armor was made for never accepted Christ. Consequently, their armor and weapons hung on the armory wall, never used.
2. They accepted Christ, but believe that spiritual armor and weapons are only an allegory, and not for real use.
3. They once were believers that had accepted Christ, but had fallen away from being in a relationship with Christ.

In the three above-listed scenarios, the armor and weapons of the marital castle occupants continued to hang on the wall until (if and when) they made the choice to get into, or back into, a relationship with Jesus Christ. The Holy Spirit confirmed my assumptions, stating, "When men and women no longer eat and drink Christ, sin creeps in, and their spiritual gifts become subdued."

Each item listed on the next page hung on the wall of the marital armory. I've listed the associated scripture for each defense mechanism, provided by the Holy Spirit. I encourage you to study this subject on your own, and become familiar with how to use the armor of God.

"Finally, be strong in the Lord and in his mighty power. Put on the full armor of God, so that you can take your stand against the devil's schemes." Ephesians 6:10-11

Daniel Touched by an Angel

"Suddenly, a hand touched me, which made me tremble on my knees and on the palms of my hands. And he said to me, 'O Daniel, man greatly beloved, understand the words that I speak to you, and stand upright, for I have now been sent to you.' While he was speaking this word to me, I stood trembling." Daniel 10:10-11 (NKJV)

God's Armor

1. Belt of Truth- *John 8:32-33*
2. Breastplate of Righteousness- *Philippians 3:9*
3. Shoes of the Gospel of Peace- *Isaiah 52:7*
4. Shield of Faith- *1 Peter 1:5*
5. Helmet of Salvation- *2 Corinthians 10:5*
6. Sword of the Spirit- *Hebrews 4:12*

"Therefore, put on the full armor of God, so that when the day of evil comes, you may be able to stand your ground, and after you have done everything, to stand. Stand firm then, with the belt of truth buckled around your waist, with the breastplate of righteousness in place, and with your feet fitted with the readiness that comes from the gospel of peace. In addition to all this, take up the shield of faith, with which you can extinguish all the flaming arrows of the evil one. Take the helmet of salvation and the sword of the Spirit, which is the word of God." Ephesians 13-17

Spiritual Gifts

While in the same vision, the Holy Spirit directed me toward the war-room. We stood in the hallway that circled the war-room, and I recall seeing the beautiful stone floors, and the craftsmanship that went into building this incredible fortress.

He said, "Before we go into the war-room, I want to show you spiritual gifts." He spoke about the talents and gifts that are assigned to men and women while in heaven—before the person is ever born.

He said, "Talents are different than spiritual gifts. Spiritual gifts are for the believer and are never recalled or retracted." He went on to say, "I assign gifts, they're not achieved through deeds. The gifts are to enhance the believer's mission or ministry while on earth, and to teach other believers. They are to be administered in love, not abused. All gifts are equally honored in standing, and assigned to build diversity within the church body. Once a believer accepts Me and starts a personal relationship with Me, they will become aware of their spiritual gift(s), and will need to use them in faith while perfecting them. Spiritual gifts are supernatural, not to be confused with Fruits of the Spirit."

He continued to explain, "Gifts of a one-flesh marriage always compliment the couple's assigned mission and purpose." I had never realized before that Stephanie and I had gifts that worked in harmony as a team, for His purpose, but we hadn't used them. I was embarrassed, and humbled, that Christ saw so much potential in us even though we failed Him so often. I was embarrassed because, as the spiritual leader of our marriage, home, and family, I should have been building on our gifts and ministry in service to Christ.

In my vision, my knees buckled underneath me. I knelt where I was standing, my hands covering my face. Tears started to roll down my cheeks, and the power of the Holy Spirit was overwhelming as He comforted me like a father or brother. He had nothing condescending to say to me, and He brought to my attention that the enemy had been working for years to destroy Stephanie and me as individuals, along with the destiny of our one-flesh relationship that was joined together by Him.

I started to see the different attacks, running through my mind like an old 8mm film with no sound. I saw the times we were spiritually attacked as children. I saw all the incidents Stephanie shared with me over the years that happened to her before I knew her. Things could have ended badly, had God not protected her.

I saw the spiritual attacks since we had been married, and I started to sob. I felt one-hundred percent unworthy to be given this vision and insight.

He said, "Your one-flesh ministry is designed to edify, assist, and heal others on their journey to find Me." He started to speak to me about how much He loved

Stephanie and me. He explained that we are precious to Him, and that Stephanie and I had been predestined to be together since before birth for this specific ministry and time of events. His hand was upon us both since we were children, and He and His angels had thwarted many attacks from the enemy over the years.

After hearing this from Him, I remained in a very humbled state of mind. My heart was full to overflowing with His love for us, and the tears continued to flow. I thought about all the mistakes I had made, how I failed and disappointed Him so many times, yet, He is so committed to us and sees our full potential. He never gives up on us or turns His back.

I said, "Please forgive me for my ignorance and disobedience." He replied, "I see no record of wrongs. You are forgiven." I sobbed even more. His mercy, grace, and forgiveness are so abundant toward us, and it was awe-inspiring to feel His love. I understood that this is how He feels for all of His children and one-flesh marriages, even the ones that deny Him.

His mercies were disguised in the last fifty years, and we didn't realize that He always came to the rescue. I stayed there for a while, soaking up the presence of the Holy Spirit before the vision ended.

Soon after, during another early-morning wakeup, the Holy Spirit said, "Ok, let's get back to it. I want you to write more about Spiritual Gifts, and time is imminent." While standing just on the edge of a larger room within the belly of the castle, He started to give me scriptures that related to spiritual gifts and Fruit of the Spirit.

Every believer is given the gift of The Holy Spirit. All spiritual gifts are the work of the Holy Spirit, and He distributes them to each one, just as He determines (1 Corinthians 12:11). Scripture tells us these gifts will never be taken away from us, as long as we follow the guidance provided in John 6:53-58. He said to write, "I want all men, women, and children to pursue their spiritual gifts and use them with maturity, boldness, and confidence to build up the church."

The Holy Spirit started to point out why it was essential to discover one's spiritual gifts. I had this sense of urgency come over me as He spoke. He said, "There are those that need to hear this and prepare. It's time My men, women, and children start studying My Word, not just reading it. They need to become humble, pray, and ask for direction. They need to trust in Me for the path I assign to them. I have given them spiritual gifts and, therefore, purpose." He went on to say, "the time is forthcoming when I will pour out My Spirit on the young and the old for the purpose of waking up and edifying the church."

Then, in what almost looked like a hologram, I started to see the words, "Spiritual Gifts" and the "Fruit of the Spirit", floating in front of me in bold, 3D high definition, coming from inside the war-room.

"In the last days, God says, 'I will pour out my Spirit on all people. Your sons and daughters will prophesy, your young men will see visions, your old men will dream dreams.'" Acts 2:17

"Now to each one, the manifestation of the Spirit is given for the common good." 1 Corinthians 12:7

Spiritual Gifts

Here's a list of the Spiritual Gifts found in Scripture:

1. The manifestation of the Spirit is for all
2. Serving
3. Teaching
4. Encouraging
5. Giving and being Generous
6. Leading
7. Mercy
8. Wisdom
9. Knowledge
10. Faith
11. Gifts of Healing
12. Miraculous Powers
13. Prophecy
14. Distinguishing Between Spirits
15. Speaking in Different Kinds of Tongues
16. Interpretation of Tongues

"We have different gifts, according to the grace given to each of us. If your gift is prophesying, then prophesy in accordance with your faith; if it is serving, then serve; if it is teaching, then teach; if it is to encourage, then give encouragement; if it is giving, then give generously; if it is to lead, do it diligently; if it is to show mercy, do it cheerfully." Romans 12:6-8

"To one there is given through the Spirit a message of wisdom, to another a message of knowledge by means of the same Spirit, to another faith by the same Spirit, to another gifts of healing by that one Spirit, to another miraculous powers, to another prophecy, to another distinguishing between spirits, to another speaking in different kinds of tongues, and to still another the interpretation of tongues. All these are the work of one and the same Spirit, and he distributes them to each one, just as he determines." 1 Corinthians 12:8-11

The Holy Spirit conveyed that He wants his one-flesh relationships to understand spiritual gifts, and to accept that He assigns gifts to every man and woman that has ever been born. With that in mind, I ask you, the reader, to start looking at your interests, the things you love to do, and the talents that get you excited. Could those be part of the spiritual gifts God has given you?

Remember that Jesus said the Holy Spirit would be our helper and comforter (John 16:7, Acts 9:31). Once you start to understand your spiritual gifts, pray for guidance and understanding. Be committed to developing your gifts through study of the scriptures. Perhaps start, or join, a ministry in your church that has similar gifts.

"...for God's gifts and his call are irrevocable." Romans 11:29

"There are different kinds of gifts, but the same Spirit distributes them. There are different kinds of service, but the

same Lord. There are different kinds of working, but in all of them and in everyone it is the same God at work." 1 Corinthians 12:4-6

"So Christ himself gave the apostles, the prophets, the evangelists, the pastors and teachers, to equip his people for works of service, so that the body of Christ may be built up until we all reach unity in the faith and in the knowledge of the Son of God and become mature, attaining to the whole measure of the fullness of Christ." Ephesians 4:11-13

"Now you are the body of Christ, and each one of you is a part of it. And God has placed in the church first of all apostles, second prophets, third teachers, then miracles, then gifts of healing, of helping, of guidance, and of different kinds of tongues. Are all apostles? Are all prophets? Are all teachers? Do all work miracles? Do all have gifts of healing? Do all speak in tongues? Do all interpret? Now eagerly desire the greater gifts." 1 Corinthians 12: 27-31

Sanctification

I started to see the word "Sanctification" in 3D, floating in the air as it crossed toward me from inside the war-room. The words "Gifts of the Spirit" floated and stayed together, as did the words "Fruits of the Spirit." As soon as I started to question why the word "Sanctification" was floating alone, it was as if the answer was gently pushed my way. The letters, about 3 feet long and at least a foot tall, passed through me as if I was invisible. I instantly knew that the Fruits of the Spirit are God's way of sanctifying us. God's intention is for all of us to achieve holiness like unto Him, and He does this through sanctification; transforming us into the image of His Son, Jesus Christ. When we seek and gain the Fruits of the Spirit, He sets into motion a process that consecrates and sets us apart. The Holy Spirit conveyed that God wants all of His people to be sanctified in body, soul, and spirit.

Fruits of the Spirit

1. Love
2. Joy
3. Peace
4. Longsuffering
5. Kindness
6. Goodness
7. Faithfulness
8. Gentleness
9. Self-Control

If we are willing to cooperate with the Holy Spirit, He will begin the sanctification process within us.

What does sanctification look like? Sanctification is a subject large enough for a book of its own, so I will not go into much detail here. However, if you start to study sanctification, the Lord will point out areas in your life that you will need to change. You may be thinking, *why should I be required to change who I am?* **The overall objective of sanctification is to make you more like Jesus**, removing ungodly traits and replacing them with Godly characteristics. If you believe change is not required, then ask the Lord to show you.

Are you up for the challenge of sanctification?

I encourage you to read Romans chapter eight, where Paul makes the excellent argument that we must make Godly choices as we live our lives, seeking to be like Christ.

- Walk according to the Spirit (8:2-4).
- Set your mind on the things of the Spirit (8:5-8).
- Death to actions of the flesh by the Spirit (8:13).
- Be led by the Spirit (8:14).
- Know the Fatherhood of God by the Spirit (8:15-17).
- Hope in the Spirit (8:23-25).
- Pray in the Spirit (8:26-27).
- Be filled with the Spirit (Eph 5:18).
- Serve in the Spirit (Rom 7:6; 15:16).
- Love by the Spirit (Rom 15:30; Gal 5:22-23; Col 1:8).

Spiritual Weapons

As the Holy Spirit took me through His Word, He often reminded that the forces of evil are not carnal, or of this world. Keep in mind that just stating your love for Jesus may not be good enough to win a battle. The conventional wisdom of the world is not enough when facing a spiritual enemy. If you're not a worshiper and doer of the Word, you are likely to lose the fight you are up against. This scripture comes to mind:

"Some Jews who went around driving out evil spirits tried to invoke the name of the Lord Jesus over those who were demon-possessed. They would say, 'In the name of the Jesus whom Paul preaches, I command you to come out.' Seven sons of Sceva, a Jewish chief priest, were doing this. One day the evil spirit answered them, 'Jesus I know, and Paul I know about, but who are you?' Then the man who had the evil spirit jumped on them and overpowered them all. He gave them such a beating that they ran out of the house naked and bleeding." Acts 19:13-16

Winning a spiritual battle is all about giving the fight to God. If you are trying to win a conflict with your will and mental capacity (strategizing, worrying, or even trying to command evil spirits through your mental toughness) you will fail. You must rely solely on God to win the battle. He has already won the war against Satan, and

He will help you win the battles. He uses us as soldiers when we are doers of the Word, and not hearers only (James 1:22).

Take some time to make a list of the troubles in your life. While free will is always at play, we need to remember that there are always spiritual forces, good and bad, at work in our lives and the lives of those around us. 99% of the circumstances that are causing you strife, whomever or whatever it be from, is not our issue or problem. Self, spouses, children, extended family, bosses, managers, neighbors, pastors, fellow saints, teachers, judges, police officers, governors, and presidents are not our enemy. Satan is the enemy. God wants us to give the battles to Him, for He is the victor against evil.

In a few paragraphs, I'll point out various spiritual weapons with which to fight the enemy. They are mighty. Seek the Lord for which weapon is appropriate for your battle.

We were recently praying about a situation with one of our daughters. We were fervently going to the Lord in prayer, seeking His guidance about what she was going through. We were concerned about the issue, and we were asking the Holy Spirit to show us how to pray about it. While waiting on the Lord to provide our next steps, Stephanie and I, along with our daughter, were sitting in a movie at a local theater.

While watching the movie, I felt the Holy Spirit come upon me. Tears started to fall. My blood felt like it was racing through my veins, but my breathing and heart were calm. All my senses were hypersensitive, and I started to get images of Esther and Mordechai from the book of Esther. The intensity continued. When Stephanie looked over at me, she asked if I was ok. I explained what was happening, and we soon left the theater. Once we were in the car, Stephanie started to read the book of Esther out loud— and in doing so, we realized that the Holy Spirit was telling us to fast for three days, just as Esther and all of the Jews in her city had done.

As soon as we got home, we felt compelled to watch the movie of Esther. That evening, we started the fast and mid-way through the third day, the Lord showed us that there had been a breakthrough, and He showed us the process that needed to be followed. We completed the fast, and the Lord provided clear direction from there.

Spiritual Weapons

Below is a list of spiritual weapons that are available to you when you are in a relationship with Jesus Christ:

1. Name of Jesus. -Col 2:15/John 14:13-14
2. Praising God and Jesus. -Psalm 8:2 and 22:3
3. Sword of the Spirit, (reading His Word). -Eph 6:17
4. Praying-(native tongue and spiritual language). -Ephesians 6:18/1- Thessalonians 5:17
5. Prayers of Binding and Loosening -Matthew 18:18
6. Fasting. -Matthew 17:21
7. Overcoming evil with good. -Rom 12:21
8. Blood of Jesus. -1 John 1:7/Revelation 12:11
9. Power of your Testimony. -Rev 12:11/Acts 1:8
10. Power of Agreement -Matthew 18:19-20
11. Intercession -Matthew 11:12/Romans 8:24
12. Anointing Oil –James 5:14
13. Assigned Angels-Hebrews 1-14/Psalms 34:7/Genesis 48:15-16

"...Forgive and act; deal with everyone according to all they do, since you know their hearts (for you alone know every human heart)." 1 Kings 8:39

"Before a word is on my tongue you, LORD, know it completely." Psalms 139:4

"He did not need any testimony about mankind, for he knew what was in each person." John 2:25

"'Yet there are some of you who do not believe.' For Jesus had known from the beginning which of them did not believe and who would betray him." John 6:64

"Knowing their thoughts, Jesus said, 'Why do you entertain evil thoughts in your hearts?'" Matthew 9:4

"...no weapon that is fashioned against you shall succeed, and you shall refute every tongue that rises against you in judgment. This is the heritage of the servants of the LORD and their vindication from me, declares the LORD." Isaiah 54:17

"Enter his gates with thanksgiving and his courts with praise; give thanks to him and praise his name." Psalm 100:4

"Truly I tell you, whatever you bind on earth will be bound in heaven, and whatever you loose on earth will be loosed in heaven." Matthew 18:18

"Again, truly I tell you that if two of you on earth agree about anything they ask for, it will be done for them by my Father in heaven. For where two or three gathers in my name, there am I with them." Matthew 18:19-20

A little over half-way through our first *Married for Life* course, we discussed praying using our spiritual language (1 Thessalonians 5:17). Our coaches made a point to help illustrate why we should pray using our spiritual language (listed as #4 in the "spiritual weapons" list.). It was profound, and made so much sense.

Have you heard the story of the Navajo Code Talkers from WWII, in the Pacific theater? In 2002, the movie *Windtalkers* was released to the big screen starring Nicolas Cage. It provided a fantastic story of how the language of the Native American Indians became pivotal during the Pacific war.

The Japanese deciphered the allied secret messages and knew most of the allied strategic moves and positions before they ever happened. Consequently, the United States and her allies suffered significant losses to the Japanese. Something had to change.

In 1940, soldiers from radio communications of the 32nd Infantry Division, started to develop a code that was undecipherable by the Japanese. The exceptional part of this story is about two groups of Native American Indians from the Chippewa and Oneida tribes. They joined the ranks of combat radio men and formed the Navajo Code Talkers. They were successful because there was a lack of written documentation on Native American Indian languages.

To make their code even more difficult to decipher, many of the same words meant multiple things. The only variance was the different pitch in sound when speaking those words. The Japanese never deciphered the code between the Navajo code talkers.

Before Stephanie and I started the *Married for Life* class in January 2018, we knew it was crucial that we pray together. However, the class went into detail about how important it was to pray in the spirit while praying together. In effect, it was speaking code to God.

Once we implemented our spirt-led prayer language as part of our daily prayer time, we immediately started to see the things we petitioned of the Lord come to pass. Changes in those we were praying for were clearly visible. Many of the repercussions of being separated for a year, on the brink of divorce, were being healed before our very eyes.

Since Satan does not have a clue what we are thinking (remember, he is not omniscient), we are essentially talking code to God when we pray in our gift of tongues. Seek your spiritual prayer language, it is a gift the Holy Spirit promises you. Pray together daily, and your one-flesh marriage will become a force not to be reckoned with. **It is extremely powerful!!**

"In the same way, the Spirit helps us in our weakness. We do not know what we ought to pray for, but the Spirit himself intercedes for us through wordless groans." Romans 8:26

"Anyone who speaks in a tongue edifies themselves, but the one who prophesies edifies the church." 1 Corinthians 14:4

"So, what shall I do? I will pray with my spirit, but I will also pray with my understanding; I will sing with my

spirit, but I will also sing with my understanding." 1 Corinthians 14:15

"God is spirit, and his worshipers must worship in the Spirit and in truth." John 4:24

"This is the confidence we have in approaching God: that if we ask anything according to his will, he hears us. And if we know that he hears us—whatever we ask—we know that we have what we asked of him." 1 John 5:14-15

Our *Married for Life* class was no joke. That twelve-week small group had a greater return of useful information, per capita, then the ten years it took to earn two master's degrees. Of course, it did! It was ordained and designed by the Holy Spirit, and given to a couple who had battled their own struggles. The key is that they listened to God and were obedient to His voice. *Married for Life* was a class of substantial value— I could tangibly see the results right before my eyes.

We made lifelong friends with other couples in the class, all of whom have struggles of their own. Friendships with like-minded, one-flesh marriages are God-approved bonds that will improve and build relationships within the church and community.

One such couple in our class was Mark and Mary— an adorable couple that we are blessed to call friends. Throughout the course, Mark and Mary had mentioned that they both had stressful commutes to work each day. Mark traveled north every morning, and Mary drove south.

During the class about Spiritual Warfare, Mary said, "I'm feeling a burden about our drive time back-and-forth to work." She asked the group for a particular prayer, focusing on protection during their commutes to work. I find it interesting that women are embedded with a power of discernment, and Mary was definitely feeling a burden about being spiritually attacked during their commutes. Stephanie and I prayed for them in our nightly prayer.

On the Friday following our class, Mark got into a car accident that blew our minds. He later explained what happened: he was driving on the interstate in a northerly direction, traveling at 65 MPH. On the opposite side of the interstate was a two-ton construction truck, traveling in the far-right, exit-only, lane. When traffic abruptly came to a halt, the driver of the truck locked his brakes to avoid hitting the car in front of him. Subsequently, it caused the driver to lose control. The truck skidded across the southbound lanes, through the median, and slammed head-on into Mark's car. Mark explained that it all happened within seconds, and he had no time to react.

He went on to describe how the Holy Spirit showed him that he was protected. He said, "Even though the crash happened in a split-second, it seemed like slow motion." I believe the Holy Spirit slowed time into fractions so Mark, and you— the reader— could experience every aspect of how He protected Mark during the crash.

Mark continued, "I could hear the sounds of metal crashing, glass breaking, and I saw the front of my car crumpling, and twisting toward me. I could feel my body thrashed around inside the vehicle, but it was like I was inside a protective bubble, watching all the carnage happen around me. The engine and all the components in the front of the car came into the driver's compartment, stopping right at my knees. My glasses were blown off my face from the airbag, but somehow, they stayed on top of my head. After the crash, I simply reached up and lowered them down over my eyes. All northbound traffic came to a screeching halt. My car was ultimately totaled, and I walked away from the crash with a small bruise on my knee, and one on my chest from the seat belt. There is no doubt the Holy Spirit protected me that day. I could feel the protection as it was happening, and it was like nothing I've ever experienced before."

He later told us that Mary found a cross with Ephesians 6:13 written on it, and it hangs by their door leading to the garage. They stop there every morning to pray together before they start their commutes.

Wow! Praise God for His protection over our friend. He is so good to us, always working on our behalf.

"Therefore, put on the full armor of God, so that when the day of evil comes, you may be able to stand your ground..."
Ephesians 6:13

The War-Room

Back in my vision of the marital castle, we left the armory and continued through a short corridor that opened into a larger room: the war-room. It was a much larger space than the armory.

I could tell we were deep under the castle, at least a couple of floors below ground level. Permission to enter the war-room was not granted to everyone in the marital castle. The Holy Spirit explained that it was granted only to those that believed in Christ and fed on His flesh and blood, as outlined in John 6:53-58.

As we stepped further into the war-room, I saw an altar on the left made of oak and hickory. The altar was like nothing I had ever seen before, carved with individual characters from biblical battles.

The ceiling was shaped like a dome, somewhat oval shaped, and was taller than an average ceiling. As I walked into the room, I noticed that the floor sloped downward toward the center. Beautiful masonry stones and tiles were everywhere. All of the floors, walls, and ceilings had breathtaking designs, created from smaller stones and tiles. There was a hallway, about four feet wide, that circled the war-room, with large and small openings into it.

From the center of the war-room, one could simply walk up the slightly-inclined floor to reach the hallway that encircled the room. Four pillars stood at each of the four directions, North, South, East, and West, curving upward and inward to join with the ceiling. The walls were lined vertically, with distinctive designs formed from beautifully-hewn stones. They extended from the floor up to the middle of the supporting pillars, then on to the center of the rounded ceiling, forming a cross. The war-room was round and had a large, round wooden table, made of— what appeared to be— oak. There were no chairs at the table, and I was given the impression that it was used for some type of briefing.

The Holy Spirit showed me that the marital castle's war-room was where the castle's occupants would determine the enemy they were facing, along with the strategy and tactics with which to fight them. Next, He showed me the protocol of the war-room.

War Room Protocol

1. I saw a man, woman, and young girl on their knees, praying at an altar. I couldn't see their faces, but I knew they were praying to the God of heaven. They were asking Him to identify the enemy, and show them how to defeat him.
2. They asked God which spiritual weapon should be used to win the battle.
3. The Lord determined the weapon and/or strategy to use.

4. The people of the marital castle would then start wielding whatever weapon was chosen by God, and allow the power of God to defeat the enemy.
5. The battle was, therefore, God's battle.

"He said: 'Listen...This is what the LORD says to you: "Do not be afraid or discouraged because of this vast army. For the battle is not yours, but God's."'" 2 Chronicles 20:15

"Be strong and courageous. Do not be afraid or terrified because of them, for the LORD your God goes with you; he will never leave you nor forsake you." Deuteronomy 31:6

"For though we walk in the flesh, we are not waging war according to the flesh. For the weapons of our warfare are not of the flesh but have divine power to destroy strongholds. We destroy arguments and every lofty opinion raised against the knowledge of God, and take every thought captive to obey Christ, being ready to punish every disobedience, when your obedience is complete." 2 Corinthians 10:3-6

"I lift up my eyes to the mountains—where does my help come from? My help comes from the LORD, the Maker of heaven and earth." Psalm 121:1-2

The Enemy Briefing

"Jesus asked him, 'What is your name?' 'Legion,' he replied, because many demons had gone into him." Luke 8:30

Still in the war-room, we moved toward the large, round table. The floor sloped slightly downward, and the ceiling sloped upward, making the room feel exceedingly large. The table was a little taller than waist high. I obediently stood at the table, waiting.

Suddenly, the enemy briefing started on what appeared to be an invisible television screen at eye level, just above the table. Regardless of where a person was standing around the table, they could all see the mysterious broadcast. The technology before me was supernatural, and I had a sense that this concept is used in heaven. Words, pictures, and videos came at a fast pace, but my mind kept up without issue. There is no way a human could process all that information at such high speeds without God's help.

The Holy Spirit started to lay out the chain of command and structure of Satan's dark forces. The Bible has confirmed there are both evil spirits and angelic beings all around us:

"For in him, all things were created: things in heaven and on earth, visible and invisible, whether thrones or powers

or rulers or authorities; all things have been created through him and for him." Colossians 1:16

We, as believers in Christ, have three significant adversaries.

1. Our Flesh (our number one enemy)
2. The World
3. Satan and his dark forces

Satan will use your flesh and the world to work against you. The solution is to walk in the spirit.

"So, I say, walk by the Spirit, and you will not gratify the desires of the flesh." Galatians 5:16

In the Bible, we learn that all things were created by the Lord (Genesis 1). It describes the creation of all things visible, like you and me, and invisible— the spiritual world of angels and demons. We're talking about a lot more than what meets the eye in this physical world on this earth. Angels and evil beings are both in the spiritual realm.

Satan's mission remains the same as it has since his fall from heaven— to steal, kill, and destroy. As with any leader, his vision is passed down to his subordinates. Evil spirits (demons) are followers of Satan, and they carry the same mission. Who do they want to steal, kill, and destroy? Those loved by God and created in His image: you and me. As mentioned earlier, anything God holds dear becomes a target for Satan to destroy.

"So, God created mankind in his own image, in the image of God he created them; male and female he created them." Genesis 1:27

"How you have fallen from heaven, morning star, son of the dawn! You have been cast down to the earth, you who once laid low the nations! You said in your heart, 'I will ascend to the heavens; I will raise my throne above the stars of God; I will sit enthroned on the mount of assembly, on the utmost heights of Mount Zaphon. I will ascend above the tops of the clouds; I will make myself like the Most High.'" Isaiah 14:12-14

"Know, therefore, that the LORD your God is God; he is the faithful God, keeping his covenant of love to a thousand generations of those who love him and keep his commandments." Deuteronomy 7:9

Satan hates you and your one-flesh marriage.

He is on "patrol" night and day, roaming the earth "seeking whom he may devour" (1 Peter 5:8, NKJV)

I'm not writing about these things to induce fear, since we all know fear and anxiety come from the devil. Instead, I write these things so you'll have knowledge and understanding to prepare for the attacks of the devil.

God, our heavenly Father, does not endorse fear. If your future looks bleak, if you fear what may happen to you, your job, your home, or anything else, know that there are over eighty verses in the Bible that discourage us from getting caught in fear's web.

Indeed, "we may boldly say, 'the Lord is my helper; I will not fear. What can man do to me?'" (Hebrews 13:6, NKJV)

Our Lord promises that no weapon formed against us will prosper. Did you hear that? No weapon. Now, believe it!!

"Even though I walk through the darkest valley, I will fear no evil, for you are with me; your rod and your staff, they comfort me." Psalm 23:4

"For the Spirit God gave us does not make us timid, but gives us power, love, and self-discipline (sound mind)." 2 Timothy 1:7

"So do not fear, for I am with you; do not be dismayed, for I am your God. I will strengthen you and help you; I will uphold you with my righteous right hand." Isaiah 41:10

Operation Secret: "Knowing Your Enemy"

The leader of the evil forces has many names: Satan, Lucifer, devil, father of all lies, dragon, the angel of darkness, (disguised as) the angel of light, the angel of the abyss, antichrist, abaddon, apollyon, beast, deceiver, liar, murderer, serpent, and son of perdition.

Don't shy away from the name of Satan, or allow yourself to feel that it's incorrect to speak his name. Satan is an evil deceiver, and *he wants to stay hidden in darkness*. He wants to keep his name, strategies, and tactics in the dark and ultimately to stay secret. When the Light shines through us, we can make the deceiver come into view and shut his mouth. Likewise, be proud to be a servant of the King of kings and Lord of lords! Be His light in the darkness while you have time (Matthew 5:14-16).

I once had the opportunity to deliberately shut Satan's deceiving mouth, and I was more than happy to do it. I was attending university in a master's program, and my professor started a discussion about how she thought people who believe in the Bible were "out there." My ears perked up. As I sat listening, I started to laugh within myself, thinking, *if she only knew what she was saying*. She continued this off-topic discussion, stating she couldn't believe some people take the Bible literally. In so many words, she was trying to tell her students that the biblical

God, Jesus, and Satan were fabrications, perhaps some type of mythology. She went further, laughing at people who believe in the rapture (a future occurrence when Jesus will come back and snatch up His saints to heaven of which I wrote about in chapter 7). She said, "Can you believe there are people that honestly believe that?"

Other students joined in, scoffing along with her. My jealousy for God and His Word started to boil within me, and I couldn't stay quiet. I stood, abruptly, and said, "I happen to be one of those people who believe the Bible is literal from the words 'Holy Bible' on the front cover, to the 'Genuine Leather' on the back. I would appreciate it if you would keep your personal opinions about my faith to yourself." She stopped talking and looked at me with big, round eyes, quickly moving on with the lesson.

By speaking up, I set myself up for failure in that class, to say the least. I had to work extra hard for a passing grade. In the end it was worth it, and I would gladly do it again. I was not going to stay quiet while my Lord and Savior was being scoffed.

Satan wants to subdue everything about God and His Word. Society is quick to judge when we mention the name of Satan as our enemy, but I encourage you, be the light of the world. Be jealous for God and His Word. Let that little light shine!!

*"'No weapon forged against you will prevail, and **you will refute every tongue that accuses you**. This is the heritage*

of the servants of the LORD, and this is their vindication from me,' declares the LORD." Isaiah 54:17 (emphasis added)

"And even as they did not like to retain God in their knowledge, God gave them over to a debased mind, to do those things which are not fitting; being filled with all unrighteousness, sexual immorality, wickedness, covetousness, maliciousness; full of envy, murder, strife, deceit, evil-mindedness; they are whisperers, backbiters, haters of God, violent, proud, boasters, inventors of evil things, disobedient to parents, undiscerning, untrustworthy, unloving, unforgiving, unmerciful..." Romans 1:28-31 (NKJV)

"They have as king over them, the angel of the abyss; his name in Hebrew is Abaddon, and in the Greek, he has the name Apollyon." Revelation 9:11

Satan's Battle Plan

Many animals, such as coyote, wolves, and lions, hunt by attempting to separate their prey from the larger group. One hunter will act as a decoy and draw the prey's attention, while other hunters will ambush them from different sides.

While in the war-room, information continued to flow as I stood at the table. I was being shown how attacks happen against us, God's children. On the other side of the veil, Satan's main objective is very similar to the strategy wild animals use to hunt their prey. They circle around us, cutting us off from our loved ones, our family, and those that care about us. *One of the enemy's greatest tactics is to isolate us.* He does this by telling us lies, instilling uncertainty, discouragement, casting condemnation for past mistakes, postponement, defeat, and *getting you to rely on yourself.* Once you are by yourself, away from God and other believers, the enemy can use your mind against you, forcing untruths and lies into your thoughts. The devil wants to steal from us, destroy us, and eventually kill us. On the next page, I have listed 12 strategies Satan uses against believers.

Satan's Strategies

1. Theft
    a. John 10:10
2. Destruction
    a. 2 Thessalonians 2:3
3. Murder
    a. John 8:44
    b. 1 John 3:12
    c. Revelation 2:10
4. Lying
    a. John 8:44
5. Strangling Faith and God's Word
    a. Mark 4:1-9
    b. Romans 10:17
    c. 1 Thessalonians 3:5
6. Blinding the Believer
    a. 2 Corinthians 4:4
7. Hiding in Sheep's Clothing
    a. 2 Corinthians 11:13-14
8. Pretending
    a. 2 Thessalonians 2:9
    b. Matthew 24:24
    c. Matthew 7:22-23
9. Tempting
    a. Matthew 4:1-11
    b. 2 Corinthians 11:3
10. Persecuting
    a. Acts 10:38
    b. Luke 13:16
    c. 1 Corinthians 12:7
11. Frustrating
    a. 1 Thessalonians 2:17-18
12. Accusing
    a. Revelation 12:10

Thinking back on our own marital situation, this makes so much sense. We started to feel isolated. We went to church by ourselves, we slept in different rooms, and eventually I left my loved ones to move over 900 miles away. I was utterly isolated in Florida. In the spiritual realm, the enemy stole the joy we had. He attempted to destroy our one-flesh marriage by separating us and convincing us that we were not a good fit for one another, when, in fact, God had appointed us to be together before we were ever born.

When a person, who usually spends time with family, suddenly starts to separate themselves, that is a possible sign that there is a spiritual war going on in their heart and mind. In my case, since the enemy thought I was spiritually dead, his next step would have been to kill me. Thankfully, I began to see the enemy's battle plan, and there was something in me that didn't want Satan to win. The amazingly good news is that *God is into resurrection and restoration.* He will restore any person, any marriage, if we only allow Him too. Christ is a healer of wounds. He takes great pleasure in forgiving, reestablishing, and reconciling relationships. What an amazing God He is! When we ask for forgiveness, He holds no condemnation for prior mistakes. They are forgotten and erased (Psalm 103:12).

Satan's Chain of Command

Still standing at the war-room table, the enemy briefing was being pumped into my mind, fast and furious. I started to see the enemy's chain of command and structure.

1. Satan (aka, "prince of the air and ruler of this world")
2. Principalities
3. Powers
4. Rulers
5. Spiritual Wickedness

"For our struggle is not against flesh and blood, but against the rulers, against the authorities, against the powers of this dark world and against the spiritual forces of evil in the heavenly realms." Ephesians 6:12

"In which you used to live when you followed the ways of this world and of the ruler of the kingdom of the air, the spirit who is now at work in those who are disobedient." Ephesians 2:2

"Now is the time for judgment on this world; now the prince of this world will be driven out." John 12:31

Satan

Beelzebub is the commander of the unbelieving, the spiritually dead. Satan is not all powerful, he was a created being originally in worship service to God. Because of his rebellion, he and the 1/3 of angels that followed him were cast out of heaven and he is now the god of this world, the god of this age, which implies that Satan controls and influences the philosophies, opinions, and views of the majority of people on earth (those that are spiritually dead). We see, in Jude 1:6, that he is the evil prince over fallen angels. He's the leader of the swarms of flies— demons which carry out repulsive, detestable, and wicked attacks against humans. His mission is to poison all things created by God. (*Ephesians 2:2, John 12:31, 2 Kings 8:24-29; 9:27; 1:2*)

Rest assured, our God is sovereign and in complete control, we have no need to fear. God has provided boundaries that Satan must operate within. Satan does not have ultimate authority, only dominion and power over nonbelievers. Jesus said He came to give sight to the blind (Luke 4:18); He was talking about unbelievers who've had their minds blinded by the darkness. That darkness is the false philosophies of the world. When people don't follow God's Word, then they're automatically part of the dark world, even when they don't think they are. Satan's philosophies are theirs, they become his prisoners. (Colossians 1:13, 2 Timothy 2:26, 1 John 5:19)

When I was in Florida, away from my family and living in sin, I would never have claimed to be on Satan's side of the war. But, since I refused to repent of my selfishness and sin against God and my wife, I was considered to be against God. I knew this, but I was delusional and kept telling myself that God had sufficient grace, that He would forgive me even if I kept sinning.

There is no in-between, we are either for Jesus Christ and following His precepts, or we belong to the son of perdition.

"Be alert and of sober mind. Your enemy, the devil, prowls around like a roaring lion looking for someone to devour." 1 Peter 5:8

"And no wonder, for Satan himself masquerades as an angel of light." 2 Corinthians 11:14

"You belong to your father, the devil, and you want to carry out his desires. He was a murderer from the beginning, refusing to uphold the truth because there is no truth in him. When he lies, he speaks his native language, because he is a liar and the father of lies." John 8:44

"This is how we know who the children of God are and who the children of the devil are: Anyone who does not do what is right is not God's child, nor is anyone who does not love their brother and sister." 1 John 3:10

"The field is the world, and the good seed represents the sons of the kingdom. The weeds are the sons of the evil one." Matthew 13:38

"Yet to all who did receive Him, to those who believed in His name, He gave the right to become children of God." John 1:12

"But he was not strong enough, and they lost their place in heaven. The great dragon was hurled down—that ancient serpent called the devil, or Satan, who leads the whole world astray. He was hurled to the earth, and his angels with him." Revelation 12:8-9

Principalities

There are three different heavens mentioned in God's Word. First, we have the heavens above the earth where birds fly, and clouds drift. (*Genesis 1:20, Job 12:7, and Psalm 8:8)*

The second heaven is where the moon, stars, and sun sit in outer space, making their treks on a celestial track like clockwork. (*Genesis 15:5, Deuteronomy 4:19, Psalm 8:3*)

Lastly, the third heaven is where God sits on His throne; where angels and believers worship Him, and where streets are made of transparent gold. This is the heaven where Jesus ascended to sit at the right hand of his Father. (*Ephesians 1:20, 2 Corinthians 12:2-4, Acts 14:19, Mark 16:19)*

A *principality* is a stronghold in the kingdom of darkness, which exists in the second heaven. Satan has assigned demons in charge of territories, continents, provinces, and dominions over the earth, to wield influence over them. The Greek root word for principalities ties back to "Arche," which means "Chief Ranking."

Now there was a day when the sons of God came to present themselves before the L<small>ORD</small>, *and Satan also came among them. And the* L<small>ORD</small> *said to Satan, "From where do you come?" So, Satan answered the* L<small>ORD</small> *and said, "From going to and fro* on the earth, and from walking back and forth on it." Job 1:6-7 (NKJV)

...in which you once walked according to the course of this world, <u>according to the prince of the power of the air</u>, the spirit who now works in the sons of disobedience. Ephesians 2:2 (NKJV, emphasis added)

For we do not wrestle against flesh and blood, but against <u>principalities</u>, against powers, against the rulers of the darkness of this age, against spiritual hosts of wickedness <u>in the heavenly places</u>. Ephesians 6:12 (NKJV, emphasis added)

Powers

Next in the chain of command are *powers*, which are given a delegated jurisdiction and authority. Powers is translated from the Greek word of *exousia* (ἐξουσία). Powers are evil forces that have satanic influence over nations. They have impact and control over regions, cities, tribes, and groups of people.

Rulers

Kosmokrator (κοσμοκράτωρ) is the Greek root word for ruler. These demons are dictatorial totalitarianism, pride, and conceit assigned to infest rulers' and dictators' hearts and minds. We can easily see it in influential world leaders such as Adolf Hitler and Joseph Stalin, along with lesser-known leaders like Jim Jones.

Spiritual Wickedness

Poneria (πονηρία) is the Greek root word for depravity. Spiritual wickedness makes up a vast majority of the demons that are in charge of the gates of hell. They are the lowest ranking of evil forces. These demons are those that make their way into the body of an unbeliever.

Those believers who work hard to keep their relationship with Jesus in check are protected from demons indwelling them.

Is it possible for believers to be possessed by a demon? Yes, because there are believers that follow 99% of Jesus teachings and decide the 1% does not apply. That 1% of sin opens doors for demons to get a foothold and eventually set up strongholds. I talk about this more in the section called, "The Enemy from Within."

The Strongmen

As I continued to watch the enemy briefing, the Holy Spirit explicitly told me to pay attention to the strongmen of this dark world. He said, "The strongmen of spiritual wickedness are commanders over many different, lower-ranking evil spirits, and they are powerful. These strongmen must be bound by prayer, and sometimes fasting, for them to be overcome." I watched and listened carefully to all that was being shown to me.

1. Unclean Spirit- *Matthew 12:43*
2. Spirit of Harlotry- *Mark 9:25*
3. Deaf and Dumb Spirit- *Mark 9:25*
4. Spirit of Infirmity- *Luke 13:11*
5. Spirit of Divination- *Acts 16:16*
6. Evil Spirit- *Acts 19:15*
7. Spirit of Bondage- *Romans 8:15*
8. Spirit of Slumber- *Romans 11:18*
9. Spirit of the World- *1 Corinthians 2:12*
10. Spirit of Antichrist- *1 John 4:3*
11. Spirit of Error- *1 John 4:6*
12. Spirit of Fear- *2 Timothy 1:7*

The Holy Spirit also showed me something interesting during the enemy briefing. I had started to develop a question regarding the scripture, "No weapon formed against you shall prosper" (Isaiah 54:17). I thought, *if no weapon will harm us, why do we even care to fight the forces of evil?*

I thought back to the vision the Lord gave me about the battlefield at Armageddon. In that vision, as we charged forward and crashed into the enemy, I could see, in detail, the up-close faces of demons. They were terrifying. They stood about 16 feet tall, and their teeth appeared to be very long and ferocious. In the vision, I was swinging the two-edged Sword of the Spirit without fear, and I was cutting down the 16-foot demons like a hot knife to cold butter. The demons were dropping like dead flies.

The Holy Spirit then explained that we have loved ones- fathers, mothers, brothers, sisters, and children- that are attacked, and if Christians do not push the enemy back in spiritual battle, those we care about, who are not believers, may lose *their* battle.

Ultimately, with God on our side, our final battle (that of making it to heaven) is won. The enemy cannot have our souls. He will, however, battle us along our journey. He wants to distract, discourage, and render us ineffective. The Holy Spirit also reminded me that we stand in the gap for other believers. While our final destination, heaven, may be assured, what are we going to do with our lives along that journey?

The briefing continued, and I learned that Satan's strongmen had smaller-ranked spirits, and they are grouped following certain strongmen spirits. For example, the demonic spirits that reports to the "Spirit of Harlotry" could be any of these lower-ranking spirits: pornography, homosexuality, confusion of God's Word, hatred of God, twisting the Truth (God's Word), pride, fornication, wounded spirit, adultery, sodomy, prostitution, lust, and rebellion.

Jesus tells us in Mark 3:27 that we need to spiritually bind demonic spirits with the authority given us through the name of Jesus, and then plunder them in their houses. Is there something in your life that you desperately wish you could break loose from? Maybe you even feel powerless in your own strength. Here's an excellent opportunity for you to take Jesus' advice and bind the strongman that has been holding you back. Start declaring victory in Jesus' name.

Sometimes we have areas in our life that we know need cleaning. The Bible tells us that we need to remove the "leaven" (sin) from our houses— clean out the cobwebs, if you will. Demonic spirits obtain a foothold in our lives by us committing sin in our thoughts and willful intentions. Little lies here and there, quick thoughts of lust over a man or woman, stealing something you may think insignificant, cursing at someone who cut you off while driving, hatred toward others, etc. All this sin develops into what I call "cobwebs of sin." Paul used the illustration of leaven, which was very pertinent in Jewish culture (1 Corinthians 5:5-7).

Mark 3:27 is so powerful. *Jesus said, "In fact, no one can enter a strong man's house without first tying him up. Then he can plunder the strong man's house."*

Jesus sets the example on how we are to take our thoughts captive, binding the strongmen of Satan who have set up strongholds in our mind and spirit. He tells us to go into the strongman's house, bind him up, and then plunder him. When an evil spirit has set up a stronghold in a person, that person becomes their house. We can't simply walk into the house, in the spirit realm, without first binding that evil spirit. However, I love the language of the King James Version:

"No man can enter into a strong man's house, and spoil his goods, except he will first bind the strong man; and then he will spoil his house."

Notice the word "spoil." In the Greek and Aramaic, spoiling means "to severely harm or damage" something. When an army invades a land to spoil it, they are destroying, burning, crushing, and throwing out everything that is of no use. Jesus tells us that, "No weapon formed against you shall prosper", because Jesus spoiled the devil and all of his weapons when He died on the cross, went to Hell, and took the keys to the gates of Hell from him.

"Truly I tell you, whatever you bind on earth will be bound in heaven, and whatever you loose on earth will be loosed in heaven." Matthew 18:18

By speaking a binding prayer over the spirit that has been holding you, or someone else, back, you effectively eliminate the threat, rendering it powerless. For example, "I bind you, spirit of addiction, in the name of Jesus." Keep in mind, God's power within you is far greater than the enemy power around you. I love 1 John 4:4 because He promises that His power is within us.

"You, dear children, are from God and have overcome them because the one who is in you is greater than the one who is in the world." 1 John 4:4

In Matthew 8:29, we witness an evil spirit recognizing Jesus as the Son of God. The spirit inquires if Jesus plans to torment him before the appointed day of judgment (Revelation 20:11-12). The evil spirit knew that the day of judgment was coming, and I'm speculating that by Jesus demanding the demon to leave the man, it would face more torture. We find that the demons went into a herd of pigs who, being so tormented, ran off a cliff.

In Luke 8:30, scriptures tell us that one man had a demon named Legion, which means 1,000. The demon confirmed this by claiming, "We are many". Some scholars believe the demon named himself Legion because the Romans had powerful legion armies at the time. Personally, I think it is possible this man had 1,000 demons in him.

Demons can also be ordered to the Abyss. I'm speculating that when they are, they're tortured for not completing their mission (which was, most likely, to torment— and eventually kill— the person they possessed).

I want to inspire you, as you build on your relationships and reinforce your castle infrastructure, to be confident in God: Father, Son (Jesus Christ), and Holy Spirit. Allow the Triune God to be your foundational support as you obtain the authority over your marital castle, by binding the strongman and kicking him out of your one-flesh marriage.

"So, Jesus called them over to him and began to speak to them in parables: 'How can Satan drive out Satan? If a kingdom is divided against itself, that kingdom cannot stand. If a house is divided against itself, that house cannot stand. And if Satan opposes himself and is divided, he cannot stand; his end has come. In fact, <u>no one can enter a strong man's house without first tying him up. Then he can plunder the strong man's house.</u>'" Mark 3:23-27 (emphasis added)

"'What do you want with us, Son of God?' they shouted. 'Have you come here to torture us before the appointed time?'" Matthew 8:29

The Enemy from Within

The Holy Spirit showed me how our flesh is the enemy from within, which works against our minds and souls.

The enemy briefing continued, showing battles for our minds and souls being launched daily, with mighty rage and ferocity. Many times, we are fighting ourselves, self being the enemy.

The Lord showed me that the parables He spoke of in His Word are for the unbeliever's thought process, presented as harmless mysteries so as not to offend them. However, when unbelievers hear the parable, there is a hidden message within it that acts as a trojan horse— so once they hear the parable, the truth slowly filters into their minds and souls without them knowing it. The truth starts to fight the battle from within. This is one of the ways Jesus searches for those who are lost.

If our minds have been defeated, and are no longer a threat to Satan and his dark forces, then we are left for dead. This is why Jesus said we must be born again. Satan's forces concentrate on the living or wounded. If we are riding the fence of the gospel, with one foot in Jesus' teachings and the other in the world, Satan considers us wounded warriors.

Allow me to explain with a hunting allegory: if you shoot two turkeys, and one falls dead immediately while the other is just wounded, which do you go after to finish the job? You go after the one that is injured, of course. The wounded one could escape or come back and peck you to death, but the dead one is finished.

Satan looks at us in the same way. If you are of the world, then you are considered a victory to Satan. If you go back and forth between following the Lord and the desires of the flesh, then you are a battle yet to be won— and Satan's #1 target. His first priority.

The enemy's outpost, entrenchment, and strongholds are established within your mind. The strongmen, demons, use the following tactics:

1. Fear (2 Timothy 1:7)
2. Worry (Matthew 6:25-27, 34; 11:28-30, Luke 12:25)
3. The lust of the mind (James 4:1)
4. The lust of the soul (1 Peter 2:11)

They use these tactics to try to get a foot-hold in your mind. By doing so, evil forces can hold the door open for other demons to pollute your thoughts.

As with Mary Magdalen, before Christ cast out the seven demons from her soul, the enemy foot-hold starts as an outpost, then develops into an entrenchment. Eventually, without spiritual intervention, they become stronghold encampments, as in the case with the demon named Legion. If we do not put on the full armor of God, including the helmet of salvation, we are subject to be attacked and claimed as victory for Satan. I don't know about you, but when I think of giving Satan an edge, my blood begins to boil, and the fighting spirit of God bursts out within me.

As you can tell from my story, I wasn't always this way. I spoke, earlier, of how I wandered for 40 years. I was on and off like a faulty electrical circuit, straddling the fence. My eyes were blinded, and the wool was pulled over my head. This allowed Satan's dark forces to make strongholds in my mind, eventually chipping away at the truth that was in me, carrying me off from my marital castle. Praise be to God, He didn't allow Satan to kill me.

If we want to win the battle for our minds, we have to take captive every ungodly thought and bind it in the name of Jesus. "Resist the devil and he will flee from you" (James 4:7). When we have mastered this spiritual warfare tactic, we can surely declare that Satan has no strongholds within our minds. We are becoming mature and experienced in Christ.

"A brother offended is harder to be won than a strong city: and their contentions are like the bars of a castle." Proverbs 18:19

"So, as the Holy Spirit says, 'Today if you hear his voice, do not harden your hearts...'" Hebrews 3:7-8

"And they took offense at him. But Jesus said to them, 'A prophet is not without honor except in his own town and in his own home.'" Matthew 13:57

"The weapons we fight with are not the weapons of the world. On the contrary, they have divine power to demolish strongholds. We demolish arguments and every pretension that sets itself up against the knowledge of God, and we take captive every thought to make it obedient to Christ. And we will be ready to punish every act of disobedience, once your obedience is complete." 2 Corinthians 10:4-6

"The God of peace will soon crush Satan under your feet. The grace of our Lord Jesus be with you." Romans 16:20

"And the devil, who deceived them, was thrown into the lake of burning sulfur, where the beast and the false prophet had been thrown. They will be tormented day and night for ever and ever." Revelation 20:10

"In the same way, the Spirit helps us in our weakness. We do not know what we ought to pray for, but the Spirit himself intercedes for us through wordless groans. And he who searches our hearts knows the mind of the Spirit, because the Spirit intercedes for God's people in accordance with the will of God." Romans 8:26-27

"Do not conform to the pattern of this world, but be transformed by the renewing of your mind. Then you will be able to test and approve what God's will is—his good, pleasing, and perfect will." Romans 12:2

"Submit yourselves, then, to God. Resist the devil, and he will flee from you." James 4:7

Godly Strategies and Tactics

Still standing at the large table in the war-room, the Holy Spirit said, "This is the last segment of the enemy briefing. Write down all the strategies and tactics I have shown you against the prince of the world and his evil forces. Those that have ears, let them hear. Those that have eyes, let them see. It is crucial my one-flesh marriages and families understand how to defend their marital castles, and destroy their enemy".

"I will not be afraid. What can mere mortals do to me?" Psalm 118:6

1. **Obedience**
    a. 1 Peter 1:14
    b. Luke 6:46
    c. John 14:15
2. **Praise**
    a. 2 Chronicles 20:2-24
    b. Psalm 150:1-6
    c. Psalm 92:1-2
3. **Reading God's Word (& Faith Visions)**
    a. Proverbs 4:7
    b. Psalm 119:105
    c. Psalm 119:130
4. **Forgiveness**
    a. Galatians 5:1
    b. Mark 11:25
5. **Praying Fervently**
    a. Psalm 138:3

        b. Matthew 26:41
6. **Fasting:**
        a. Esther 4:11-17
        b. Daniel 9:3
7. **Sowing**
        a. 2 Corinthians 9:6-11
        b. Psalms 126:4-6
8. **Selflessness**
        a. Matthew 25:40
        b. Philippians 2:2-4
        c. Hebrews 13:16
        d. Acts 20:35
9. **Binding and Loosening**
        a. Matthew 16:19
        b. Matthew 18:18
        c. Luke 13:12
10. **Abstain from every form of evil**
        a. 1 Thessalonians 5:22
        b. Proverbs 4:15

"You are all children of the light and children of the day. We do not belong to the night or to the darkness. So then, <u>let us not be like others,</u> <u>who are asleep, but let us be awake and sober</u>. For those who sleep, sleep at night, and those who get drunk, get drunk at night. But since we belong to the day, let us be sober, putting on faith and love as a breastplate, and the hope of salvation as a helmet. For God did not appoint us to suffer wrath but to receive salvation through our Lord Jesus Christ. He died for us so that, whether we are awake or asleep, we may live together with him. Therefore encourage one another and build each other up, just as in fact you are doing so." 1 Thessalonians 5:5-11 (emphasis added)

"<u>Do not quench the Spirit.</u> Do not treat prophecies with contempt but test them all; hold on to what is good, reject every kind of evil. May God himself, the God of peace, sanctify you through and through. May your whole spirit, soul, and body be kept blameless at the coming of our Lord Jesus Christ. The one who calls you is faithful, and he will do it." 1 Thessalonians 5:19-24 (emphasis added)

"Be alert and of sober mind. Your enemy, the devil, prowls around like a roaring lion looking for someone to devour. Resist him, standing firm in the faith, because you know that the family of believers throughout the world is undergoing the same kind of sufferings." Peter 5:8-9

The Fourth Watch

The inspiration and drive for this book started in the *Married for Life* course that Stephanie and I first attended in late January, 2018. Writing this book took over a year, and most of the visions I received from the Holy Spirit occurred during the fourth watch. Has the Lord been waking you at the fourth watch? I've outlined the different watch periods below.

In ancient Jewish days, the time period between dusk to dawn, 6 PM to 6 AM, was broken down into three parts. When the Romans came on the global scene, they changed it to four watches. Men would stand guard over their families, tribes, and cities to keep them safe and secure during the different watches.

1. First Watch: 6-8:59 PM
2. Second Watch: 9-11:59 PM
3. Third Watch: 12-2:59 AM
4. Fourth Watch: 3-6 AM

We find in scripture that the fourth watch was a strategic time the Lord used often. In one example, the Lord commanded King Saul to attack the Ammonites during the fourth watch. We can assume there is strategic value to this period of early morning.

There is validity to the 4th watch. From my Army days, I learned that the Army Rangers practice an ancient method adopted by Native American Indians. There is a time period that is called, "Before Morning Nautical Twilight," which is about thirty minutes, to an hour, before dawn. History tells us that Colonel Roger's Rangers, of the American colonial army, would be in defensive positions with 100% of the men at the ready well before dawn, because of Native American Indian attacks (US Army Ranger Handbook, 1985, ii). We also see this during the battle of Point Pleasant (Dunmore's War), Virginia now West Virginia (Westholme 2018).

I pointed out earlier that the physical and spiritual worlds operate parallel to one another. Satan uses people, just like God does, to complete his missions. On the whole, people are typically fast asleep during the fourth watch. I believe this specific period of time is when the dark forces of evil may be resting as well, or at least engaged in low demonic activity.

The Lord moves during the Fourth Watch

- 1 Samuel 11:11 – newly-appointed King Saul, filled with the Holy Spirit and burning with the anger of the Lord, attacked Nahash of the Ammonites during the fourth watch, obtaining victory.

- Genesis 32:22-31 – Jacob wrestled with God, meeting Him face to face, just before being renamed Israel.
- Exodus 14:24-26 – Moses led the Israelites across the Red Sea.
- Judges 7:19-24 – Gideon defeated the Midianites (middle watch).
- Matthew 14:25-26 – Peter and Jesus walked on water.
- Matthew 25:1-13 – the bridegroom returned for His bride in the night hours.
- Luke 2:8-14 – the angels appeared to the shepherds in the field to announce the birth of the Savior.
- Matthew 26:40-45 – Jesus urged the disciples to pray, just before He was arrested.
- Matthew 28:1 – Jesus resurrected from the dead.

From these examples, we can see that the Lord uses the fourth watch to break through evil spiritual activity. He also warns us to be watching during that time.

"Be dressed ready for service and keep your lamps burning, like servants waiting for their master to return from a wedding banquet, so that when he comes and knocks, they can immediately open the door for him. It will be good for those servants whose master finds them watching when he comes. Truly I tell you, he will dress himself to serve, will have them recline at the table and will come and wait on them. It

will be good for those servants whose master finds them ready, even if he comes in the middle of the night or toward daybreak. But understand this: If the owner of the house had known at what hour the thief was coming, he would not have let his house be broken into. You also must be ready, because the Son of Man will come at an hour when you do not expect him." Luke 12:35-40

I want to encourage you, if you find yourself mysteriously waking at the top of the hour between 2-6 AM (the Jewish third watch, or Roman fourth watch) consider it a blessing. Get up and pray. Worship the Lord. You will find this time to be very powerful and rewarding.

Recently, while praying during the fourth watch, the Holy Spirit spoke to me and identified three evil spirits at work in a person I was praying for. He also showed me which was the weakest, which was second in command, and the demonic spirit that had the most influence over the person. I took guidance from the Holy Spirit on how to pray for this person, and spoke the name of Jesus over and over as that person came to mind.

As I continued to speak the name of Jesus, I could feel the battle raging in the spiritual realm. Something in me commanded me to continue to say the name of Jesus without ceasing. I continued to pray and bind those evil spirits in Jesus' Name. The only power I had was the name of Jesus. Oh, what power is in that name! I heard footsteps, as of the demon leaving the person. The Lord later confirmed, through another believer, that those spirits had left that person.

Our Spiritual Victories

I felt it essential to write a few short story testimonies regarding the spiritual battles we've won. I believe these true stories will show how faithful and committed God is to one-flesh marriages. You can take comfort in the fact that, when these events took place, we didn't fully know how to use our spiritual weapons against Satan. Thankfully, our knowledge has grown in this area, and yours can, too. If God and the Angels were fighting for us when we lacked understanding, how much more powerful can our one-flesh be through the knowledge Jesus provides us through His Word? I pray these testimonies speak to your heart, and show how your spiritual weapons can work for you and your family.

A German Fall

It was August, 1986. Stephanie and I had been married just over a year, and we lived in Nurnberg, Germany. We had lived there for about a year when we were both attacked.

Before I go any further, I need to explain that since the age of fifteen, I'd had voices telling me I would never live past 21 years old. I shared this with very few people, but I did tell Stephanie this dreadful statement when we were getting to know each other at age 17. From time to time, those same voices would mock me, hatefully telling me, "I'm coming for you," or, "You'll never live past 21 years old." I started to believe it.

Stephanie and I both turned 21 while in Germany in 1986. I was in the Army, where my unit did a lot of ranger operations and mountaineering training. Stephanie's mother was having surgery in August, so she flew home to be with her. While she was in the United States, I fell 70 feet off a cliff while repelling in Pottenstein, Germany. My injuries were incredible. My pelvis was broken in seven places, multiple ribs were broken, my urethra was severed in two locations, my liver was lacerated, my lungs collapsed, my diaphragm and spleen were both ruptured. I was medevac'd by helicopter to a German hospital, where exploratory surgery ensued.

Meanwhile Stephanie, still in the United States, was notified that I was in intensive care in Bayreuth, Germany, not sure if I would live. She quickly returned to Germany, traveling four hours a day to visit me in the hospital. I had no idea of the pressure and stress she was experiencing. She was in a foreign country, newly married, only twenty-one years old—and not knowing if I would live or ever walk again. It took a toll on her health.

Eventually, the Army transferred me to the American Army hospital in Furth, Germany, which was about a fifteen-minute drive from our apartment on Ruprecht Strasse. I woke one morning to find I had been moved from a large room, with several beds, to a double room. I looked over and found Stephanie in the bed next to me. She had been admitted to the hospital with a spontaneous pneumothorax, a collapsed lung, the third time this happened in her life. Many thought we were victims of a car crash.

Meanwhile, back in the United States, prayer warriors were hard at work. My mother, my grandmother, my family, and Stephanie's mom and family, were all praying for us. My grandmother, Caroline, was on her death bed. She told my mother that the Lord visited her, and explained that we would be completely healed. She died before I was conscious enough to know she was even sick. Caroline wrote a message about this on a small piece of paper in her Bible, placing it on the same page as John 15:7. The Bible scripture she received from the Holy Spirit was, *"If ye abide in me, and my words abide in you, ye shall ask what ye will, and it shall be done unto you."* John 15:7 (KJV)

Stephanie healed and was released from the hospital a few weeks later. After many surgeries, I was released and returned to active duty in July of 1987, almost exactly a year later, with no significant issues. The Army would have never allowed me to stay on active duty if I couldn't pass the Army physical fitness test; a 2-mile run, sit-ups, and pushups.

One year after my fall from a cliff, 70 feet straight down, with a pelvis that was crushed and broken in seven places, I passed the Army Physical Fitness Test. Four years later, I was repelling out of helicopters, and six years later I was jumping out of airplanes and running four to six miles a day. Stephanie never had another spontaneous pneumothorax, and I successfully ended my Army career after twenty years. I believe, without a doubt, my grandmother, our mothers, and prayers from family turned this critical situation around. I promised to tell it wherever I go. Praise be to God!!

First Major Attack on our Children

While Stephanie and I were stationed at the 101st Airborne Division, in Fort Campbell, Kentucky, we experienced an attack on our oldest daughter. She was two and a half years old at the time. Our sweet girl started complaining one evening that her tummy was in pain. Thinking it was constipation or gas, we repeatedly attempted to assist her to the bathroom so she could relieve herself. Nothing worked, however, and the pain escalated with every passing minute. Her stomach was hard as a rock. She began to have spasms every few minutes, letting out blood-curdling screams of agony, which expressed her excruciating pain. Around 10 PM, we rushed her to the emergency room. Of course, the waiting room was jammed packed, and the ER was understaffed. We waited for about an hour, and every few minutes she would let out long screams. We could tell it was a severe health situation, and we started to panic. I went to the desk and demanded someone look at her, since we could tell things were escalating with each passing minute, and we feared her intestines or stomach would burst. I threatened to take her to a civilian hospital if they didn't see her soon.

They could see the desperation in our faces, and the doctors sent her for an x-ray of her abdomen. When Stephanie and our daughter returned from the x-ray, nothing had changed, her screams coming just a minute apart. Stephanie and I were desperate. We thought our daughter would die in our arms in the waiting room. Finally, I picked up our daughter and started to pace with her, since she was now screaming at the top of her lungs in pain. I was standing between the receptionist desk and the jammed-pack waiting room. Stephanie came to stand with us, and we held each other, her crying, and we started praying silently and desperately.

Up until that point, I kept my faith hidden and would never express it in public. However, I thought, *if praying out loud will get His attention, then I'll do it*. I prayed right there, out loud, with Stephanie joining in. We prayed that Jesus would heal her, that her pain would go away, and that it would never come back. When we were done praying, I looked at the people in the waiting room, and saw the concern in their eyes as well. Our daughter then caught our attention with, "Mommy, I need to go to the bathroom." Stephanie rushed her into the bathroom, and moments later, they came out— my precious little one was feeling much better. Not long after, the doctor took our daughter back to the ER and examined her. After many pushes on her belly, with no pain, they released her and we got to go home.

At 4:00-5:00 the next morning, we received a call from a panicked radiologist who demanded we rush our daughter back to the ER. Stephanie scooped our little one up and was there in minutes. The doctors reexamined her and still found nothing. The radiologist explained that the x-ray showed her intestine had telescoped, and was on the verge of bursting. He went further to tell us if they would have realized the results of the x-ray while at the hospital, they would have performed emergency surgery. If we had not said our first one-flesh prayer over our oldest daughter, she would likely have not made it that night. Praise be to God!

"Whoever acknowledges me before others, I will also acknowledge before my Father in heaven." Matthew 10:32

"For where two or three gathers in my name, there am I with them." Matthew 18:20

"And I will do whatever you ask in my name, so that the Father may be glorified in the Son. You may ask me for anything in my name, and I will do it." John 14:13-14

The Attack at Disney

Another attack was against our seven-year-old son in May of 2009. We took a week-long family vacation to Walt Disney World in Florida. We had decided to fly to Florida and use Disney transportation to get around, so we didn't have any vehicle of our own. We had the whole family on the trip; Stephanie and I, our two daughters, our son, and Stephanie's mom.

We dropped our bags at the room as soon as we arrived at the Caribbean Beach Resort. My son was eager to head to the pool, so he and I went for about an hour while the girls unpacked the bags and Stephanie decorated the pirate-themed room with pirate toys and stuffed animals. Once we made it back to the room, our entire group set out on a short walk to the resort bus stop, with plans to travel to Downtown Disney where we would validate our park tickets. Our plan was to then catch a bus to the Wilderness Lodge for dinner reservations.

We surprised our son with a small plastic sword from the Pirates of the Caribbean theme. As we were walking to the bus, he kept tossing the sword up in the air. He and I were a little quicker than the girls, so we managed to get ahead of them. On his last toss, the sword landed about a foot off the sidewalk, in a bed of flowers and large, leafy plants. I kept looking back to ensure the girls were keeping up with us.

Before I knew it, my son was standing directly in front of me, yelling in a frantic voice, "Daddy, daddy, daddy," to get my attention. I looked down at my three-foot-tall boy to see what was so urgent. As he pushed his bloody hand up toward my face, he said, "Something bit me." I was astonished and wondered; *what animal would bite him at Disney? Maybe he just snagged his hand on a prickly plant of some sort.* I looked closer and could see something had, indeed, bitten him on his fingers and thumb. I assured him it would be okay, because he seemed to be on the edge of crying. I then asked him to show me where he had put his hand. As soon as I looked to where he pointed, I saw a black and brown snake lounging on a large plant, watching us.

I held my son close to me and tried to get the attention of the girls. They were walking on the sidewalk coming toward us, but they were still fifty yards away. He did not see the snake and wasn't sure what had caused all the blood. I yelled out to the girls to come quick. However, they continued to walk and chat. I then yelled out, "He's been bitten by a snake!" Stephanie replied, "What? Oh, sweet Jesus!" and came running.

All the girls showed up with concern and started looking at the snake. My oldest daughter, who loves photography, attempted to take pictures of the snake and was able to get a good look at it. The snake knew he was in trouble and quickly slithered down the plant, deeper into the vegetation, and away from us. We had only been at Disney for about two hours.

Stephanie picked up and cradled our precious boy, assuring him everything would be ok. I called 911, requested assistance, and asked that he be checked out at the resort bus stop by an ambulance. Stephanie's spiritual instincts kicked in, and she started praying over our son in her spiritual language. She prayed loudly and confidently, not afraid of who might hear her. I continued to speak to resort and emergency officials as they were approaching our bus stop. We left the sword just off the path where it fell so we could show park officials where the accident had happened.

While waiting for the paramedics, Stephanie continued to hold and cradle our son, all the while praying for him. At this point, he became panicked due to the excruciating pain, and began screaming. He asked her a few times, "Mommy, mommy, am I going to die?" and "Did you see its tail?" Being an avid fan of animal planet, he wanted to know if it was a rattle snake. Of course, Stephanie confidently reassured him he would be fine.

Once the paramedics arrived, they guaranteed us that everything would be ok. They cleaned the blood off his hand and fingers and bandaged him up. They commented that we didn't need to take him to the emergency room, and we should later visit Urgent Care as a follow-up because snakes have a lot of bacteria in their mouths. Stephanie said, "We don't have transportation here. If this was your family member, what would you do?" Her protective momma instincts, along with her spiritual awareness, were in overdrive. The paramedics heard the concern in her voice and agreed to take him to the hospital in Celebration, Florida. As soon as the ambulance doors opened upon reaching the hospital, the ER surgeon met them at the back of the ambulance to take a look at the bite. The doctor said, "You're going to be with us for a while. That bite was from a venomous snake."

Stephanie called me, explaining what the doctor said. The girls and I rushed back to the resort office and requested a ride to the hospital. The girls started to search the internet in hopes of identifying the snake, but it wasn't until we got to the hospital, with help from our future son-in-law, that we determined the snake was a Cottonmouth, also known as a Water Moccasin. The doctors explained that the snake struck him three times on his fingers and thumb, and that they needed to admit him to the pediatric intensive care unit. Within a couple of hours, the doctors determined he was too sick to be treated at the Celebration Hospital and transferred him to the Florida Children's Hospital.

We started our spiritual warfare counter-attack when Stephanie called the girl's youth pastor in Kentucky. We sounded the alarm at the marital castle and sent a text to everyone we knew, asking for prayer. Our boy's life was in jeopardy, and he didn't have much time. Pictures, along with the story, were posted on Facebook and went viral in no time. Because we were a military family, many of our friends were located in different parts of the world, which meant we had people around the world praying for our son's healing.

The doctors at Florida Children's Hospital were alarmed when they found that antivenin (Crofab) had not been started right away by Celebration Hospital. We learned later that they hadn't administered antivenin treatments because they felt it would cause more damage, based on his age. When our son was admitted to the oncology intensive care unit, he was considered their sickest patient. During his three-day stay, he received antivenin treatments costing more than $140,000. We watched in horror as the physicians tracked the venom and infection as it traveled up his arms toward his heart. They sketched rings on his wrist, then forearm, bicep, and lastly his shoulder with a black permanent marker. As we watched the venom travel up his arm each day, we prayed even harder. On the third day, the doctors commented that his hand should have turned black, and possibly result in him losing his right hand.

On the evening of the third day, our son was released from the hospital feeling a little nauseous, in a wheelchair, and with his arm in a sling. We extended our stay at Walt Disney World, as he continued to gain more strength in his body each day. His hand never turned black, his fingers were never disfigured, and he was completely healed.

When our son was eight-years-old, he taught himself how to play two songs from, beginning to end, on a keyboard. When he turned nine, we bought him a used piano for his birthday. He is now seventeen years old and writes lyrics, music, and is working on his first album. In hindsight, we believe the enemy was trying to steal, kill, and destroy our son's musical gifts and anointing. Praise be to God for answering prayers and healing him from this attack.

"Heal me, O Lord, and I will be healed; save me, and I will be saved, for you are the one I praise." Jeremiah 17:14

"So do not fear, for I am with you; do not be dismayed, for I am your God. I will strengthen you and help you; I will uphold you with my righteous right hand." Isaiah 41:10

A Siege on our Youngest Daughter

The Bible tells us that the enemy knows who we are, even when we are in a relationship with Christ. The dark forces of hell understand that we have spiritual gifts assigned to us at birth. Perhaps they even know the full potential God sees in us. Some people are mildly assaulted during their life, while others are under siege for long periods, or even their entire life. Satan knows every person God created, he can see us through the spiritual veil. Some are bigger threats to the dark forces than others. I feel the greater spiritual potential a person has, the harder the enemy will fight them. An excellent example of this theory is the apostle Paul. Acts 19:15 tells us that the demons knew who Paul was. They knew him because he was a spiritual threat to their existence. Another example is Job. He was a fantastic, godly servant of the Lord, and Satan wanted to devour him because he desires to destroy all that which is excellent to God. Satan took everything from Job and caused incredible havoc and destruction in his life (Job 1:6-12; 2:3-6).

The point is, Satan knew who Job was because he loved and served God. We can see demonic forces targeted both Paul and Job because of their godly influence on others. When godly people want to make the kingdom of God prevail on earth, we know that Satan is going to do everything in his power to destroy, steal, or kill that person. The good news is that, because of Jesus Christ's sacrifice for us, Satan's evil forces have no ultimate control over us as long as we are in a strong relationship with Christ. However, when you are not, you open the door for the strongholds in your mind and life to be taken over by the forces of hell.

When our youngest daughter was about eight years old, she joined a Bible quiz team at our church. We realized her ability to memorize, verbatim, many chapters and books of the Bible. As a child, she was prophesied over to have a gift of prophecy.

We noticed that strong evil forces crept into her life and laid siege to her. Connecting socially with other children started to become a challenge. Soon after, fear and anxiety gripped her to the core. We noticed an escalation in her anxiety when I deployed to Iraq in 2003. She started to believe fear and anxiety were just part of her life.

The enemy lied to her, and convinced her that there was something wrong with her ability to socially connect with others. She started to believe it, and she struggled to make friends. Although she managed to get through high school, she would become anxious about meeting with other people.

It was around this time that she was diagnosed with depression. She felt content academically, but she didn't like the social aspect of school. This caused her to become sick, to simply avoid people. When she prepared to go to college, she felt that it would be a fresh start, and didn't think the anxiety of seeing people would resurface. She completed her first year in college, but we had to stay in constant contact with her.

During her third semester, we kept in frequent communication with her to mitigate any issues that might develop with her depression. Everything had been going well, but in 2014, while living at the university, she suddenly stopped returning texts and calls. After Stephanie finally reached her by phone, we realized she was in a crisis. We made an emergency trip to the university, praying all the way there, and found her in bed in the middle of the day. She had been in bed, without much to eat or drink, for about a week. We packed her up that day and brought her home.

In 2015, being severely depressed, she started having suicidal thoughts, complete with a plan of execution. We prayed many times that she would be rescued from depression, but the enemy had her in a choke hold, and under siege. She was so sad and unhappy about her life, and she didn't want to live. Because of her mental state, we were forced to check her into the hospital. She spent three days in the hospital and received much-needed care. She was continually tormented with depression from 2003 to early 2018.

Why the siege on our precious girl? Why are some under siege, and others not? What could be the difference? We believe this brilliant, beautiful girl of ours has a strong calling on her life, and the strongmen have been after her to prevent all the great things she would, and will, do for the kingdom of God. When asked when she started to feel better, she admitted, "In early 2018".

Looking back, she realized she was feeling altogether happier now. We immediately recognized a significant parallel that lined up with early 2018: Stephanie and I were in our first *Married for Life* course during that time. The course taught us how to pray for our family and conduct spiritual warfare. In February of 2018 was when we started praying together in the spirit daily. Since then, we actively started to see her become the bright-eyed, beautiful woman God created her to be.

"Be alert and of sober mind. Your enemy, the devil, prowls around like a roaring lion looking for someone to devour. Resist him, standing firm in the faith, because you know that the family of believers throughout the world is undergoing the same kind of sufferings." 1 Peter 5:8-9

We Fortified Our Castle

As Stephanie and I started to look at the attacks I've written about in previous pages, we began to see a pattern. The pattern was related to one of us having sin in our lives at the time. I admit, 99% of the time it was me, as I have struggled with sin most of my life. However, the picture is crystal clear, and turning away from our relationship with Christ is no longer an option for either of us.

Since our first *Married for Life* class in early 2018, we have been reading the word, worshipping, and praying together every evening, taking our petitions and concerns to the Lord. Recently, while Stephanie and I were praying, the Holy Spirit conveyed that our one-flesh marriage was protected from any attacks at the moment because of the condition of our relationship with Christ. So, I asked the question, "Lord, how do we get the same protection for our children?" He immediately replied, "Bring them into your daily prayer circle." After that, I received an image of Stephanie and me with our children, holding hands and praying together.

He said, "When the spiritual leaders of the marital castle have lukewarm relationships with Christ, the enemy can, and will, attack." He went on to say, "When children become of age to make their own decisions, and act on what is right or wrong by My Word, they are accountable for their actions." We can be intercessors for our children, helping ward off enemy attacks and win battles.

As we walk with Christ, future attacks are going to come. **The important difference in the matter <u>is staying intimate with Christ</u>, so that no weapon that the enemy forms against us will ever prosper**.

However, until our loved-ones turn from sin, and follow Christ, making Him the center of their life, they will be vulnerable to future enemy attacks.

"I have told you these things, so that in me you may have peace. In this world, you will have trouble. But take heart! I have overcome the world." John 16:33

Chapter 10

Fortifications and Defenses

While in prayer one morning, I found myself in another vision, high on a great stone wall of the marital fortress. In this particular vision, it was evening of a beautiful day. I could hear birds chirping, cows mooing, and sheep off in the distance. I felt the beams of light coming through the clouds, almost like high-beam spotlights at a football stadium. On my right, inside of this fantastic fortress, I could see small gardens and people leading horses, going about their day. On my left, outside the fortress walls, were trees and delightful landscapes as far as I could see. There were also blue lakes and white streams off in the distance. Everything I saw was so crystal clear and beyond belief, as if time had slowed down to allow me to take it all in.

The Holy Spirit cautioned me, "Although this is a mighty fortress, it can— and will— be attacked." He went further, "The one-flesh marriage must stay vigilant. The man and woman must keep their relationship intimately united in agreement with Me as they patrol their fortifications. They must use discernment and prayer while watching and waiting for the enemy attack, because the enemy *will* attack."

The information kept pouring in, and I could feel that the words being spoken were somehow being seared into my memory for later use. I started to think about how Stephanie and I pray, and have been praying vigilantly, since God reconciled our marriage.

We have adopted a strategic prayer life since our first *Married for Life* class. We pray together each night just before going to bed, and we alternate who leads the prayer. One of us will pray in our natural language, while the other will pray in their spiritual language. We petition the Lord for guidance, discernment, a protective hedge over our children and grandchildren, our finances and investments, etc. We have been praying in this manner every night since February 2018, and we've seen amazing answers to prayer as the Spirit moves on our behalf.

We have our own personal devotion times with Christ, and we pray individually about things we feel impressed to bring before the Lord. We both fear God and desire an intimate relationship with Christ.

Shortly after beginning the *Married for Life* class, we both felt drawn to become involved in that amazing ministry. This mutual feeling was later confirmed, when our leaders shared with us that the Holy Spirit had shown them that we would be a leader couple, information that was revealed to them before they even knew who we were. As Stephanie often says, this class is a game-changer. It has forever altered the trajectory of our lives, not only within our own marriage, but also with our one-flesh ministry.

When I say we have been through the depths of despair, I am not kidding. When I say God has been incredibly gracious with His redemptive love, my heart is beyond thankful. God has taken what the enemy meant for evil, and has turned it around for His glory.

Stephanie and I are now leaders in the *Married for Life* Ministry.

Back to the vision: as I stood there on the walls of that strong fortress, I felt the strength of it was reinforced by none other than God. I sensed that the fortress, and the lands around it, were blessed by the Creator Himself. Imagine that! The Creator of the universe cares so much about us that He personally upholds our marriages and relationships. When a man and woman are in covenant with each other and God, then the fortress becomes even more powerful and robust, compared to those who are not in the same covenant.

The Holy Spirit brought to mind Psalm 46. He said, "Write how I am a mighty fortress, a helper, and a protector to those who trust Me."

"God is our refuge and strength, an ever-present help in trouble. Therefore, we will not fear, though the earth gives way and the mountains fall into the heart of the sea, though its waters roar and foam and the mountains quake with their surging. There is a river whose streams make glad the city of God, the holy place where the Most High dwells. God is within her, she will not fall; God will help her at break of day. Nations are in uproar, kingdoms fall; he lifts his voice, the earth melts. The LORD Almighty is with us; the God of Jacob is our fortress.

Come and see what the LORD has done, the desolations he has brought on the earth. He makes wars cease to the ends of the earth. He breaks the bow and shatters the spear; he burns the shields with fire. He says, 'Be still, and know that I am God; I will be exalted among the nations, I will be exalted in the earth.' The LORD Almighty is with us; the God of Jacob is our fortress."
Psalm 46

    I could see the trees gently blowing, and I smelled a new fragrance as the wind blew something fresh and satisfying toward me. In the distance, the form of a white cloud appeared to be coming in my direction, and I somehow knew that it would have a pleasant aroma.

    I was two or three stories above the ground, still on the castle walls and behind embattlements. The white cloud came closer, now appearing to be a floating ribbon of white, coming directly at me. As it grew closer, the cloud transformed into a banner. The fabric of the banner was the width of a bed sheet, the length was about fifty yards long. There were words written on it.

    Gliding on the wind, like a hot-air balloon, the banner came directly toward me. The Holy Spirit told me to be still and watch. Just before it reached me, I saw titles saying; "Roles of Husband and Wife," "One-flesh Concepts," "Power of Synergism," "One-flesh Purpose," "One-flesh Ministry," "One-flesh Maintenance," "One-flesh Security," "Patrol Hedges," and, lastly, "One-flesh Plan." I remembered that these titles were topics we had learned about during our *Married for Life* class.

As the sizeable white ribbon started to overtake me, I took a long, deep breath. As I was breathing in the words, I could feel my lungs and body become exhilarated and refreshed. I stretched out my arms and arched my back, in order to deeply inhale the ribbon of words into my lungs. I knew I didn't want any of the information to get past me, so I inhaled as much of the information as I could. As I inhaled the words, something was telling me that they were taken from God's truth, and He wanted all marriages to know them.

When the Holy Spirit told me to take all He had shown me and write it down, He said, "My church is sleeping, and it is time for recalibration. I'm getting ready to pour out My Spirit, and Satan will retaliate in anger. We are in the last hour, and My one-flesh marriages need to prepare. Wake them up!" That statement alone has been driving me, day and night, to complete this book.

I sensed everything the Holy Spirit wanted to show me about the marital castle was coming to an end. I boldly asked Him, "Who owns this amazing castle?" He immediately took me back to the vision of the two generational lines of people, working together to lay the stone of the castle (I wrote about that part of the vision in the *inner-keep* section of chapter six).

In this vision, however, I was on a different, though sizeable, flat rock, elevated high above the trees, with sheer cliffs all around. I could see the valleys, lakes, and streams for miles. Rays of sunshine shone down, and I saw Stephanie and myself leading the same generational lines of people that I had seen in the previous vision. This time, I could see their faces. As we laid stone, we were working side-by-side with the parents of our daughters' and son's spouses, and their generational lines. I looked over my shoulder and saw our parents, their parents, and their parents before them, all passing stones, one-by-one, to us, so we could lay stones for our children, grandchildren, and future generations. I thought about what I was seeing. The Lord confirmed my growing suspicion: the generational lines I had seen in the previous vision were laying the stone for my and Stephanie's marital castle.

He said, "This marital fortress is just one of many within My kingdom. I want all of my one-flesh marriages to align with My Word. Everything I have shown you is about the marital castle of Julian and Stephanie Adkins." I was speechless. This realization was incredibly humbling.

My body shook as I bowed my head, and tears refused to be held back. Completely overwhelmed with His presence and love for us, I felt totally unworthy of all He had done for our marriage over the years. I thought about how I was probably on God's list for one of the worst husbands of all of time. I wondered, *why did He pick me as His messenger, to show me all these visions of the marital castle?* He immediately responded, "Because you said, 'here I am, Lord.'"

I started to scan my memory for everything I had seen: the lush green crops, lakes of blue, streams of white, and the beautiful masonry and woodcarvings of the mighty fortress. I remembered the stone passage to the armory, the spiritual weapons, the spiral stairs leading to the magnificent paintings on the ceiling, and the tapestry of the great hall. Lastly, I thought about the generations of labor and sweat that went into building the marital castle, and how important it was to defend it at all cost, and keep it beautiful.

The vision ended, and I found myself on my knees.

"He who dwells in the secret place of the Most High shall abide under the shadow of the Almighty. I will say of the LORD, 'He is my refuge and my fortress; My God, in Him I will trust.' Surely, He shall deliver you from the snare of the fowler and from the perilous pestilence. He shall cover you with His feathers, and under His wings you shall take refuge; His truth shall be your shield and buckler. You shall not be afraid of the terror by night, nor of the arrow that flies by day, nor of the pestilence that walks in darkness, nor of the destruction that lays waste at noonday. A thousand may fall at your side, and ten thousand at your right hand; But it shall not come near you. Only with your eyes shall you look, and see the reward of the wicked. Because you have made the LORD, who is my refuge, Even the Most High, your dwelling place, No evil shall befall you, nor shall any plague come near your dwelling; For He shall give His angels charge over you, To keep you in all

your ways. In their hands they shall bear you up, lest you dash your foot against a stone. You shall tread upon the lion and the cobra, the young lion and the serpent you shall trample underfoot. 'Because he has set his love upon Me, therefore I will deliver him; I will set him on high, because he has known My name. He shall call upon Me, and I will answer him; I will be with him in trouble; I will deliver him and honor him. With long life I will satisfy him, and show him My salvation.'" Psalm 91 (NKJV)

With Jesus Christ intimately in our hearts, minds, and souls, we shall live happily ever after.

The End

Annexes of the Marital Castle

Stephanie's Faith Vision

I'm sharing the original faith vision Stephanie found for our marriage at faithandmarriageministries.org. She simply filled in the blanks with my name and prayed this prayer every day.

Faith Vision for Marriage

I thank you, Lord, that _____ lives with me in considerate understanding and respect for my role as his wife and that his prayers will not be hindered. 1 Peter 3:7. I praise You that everything we have been through has not quenched his love for me, and neither have floods or rivers washed it away. Song of Solomon 8:7 and that he does not feel harsh, bitter or resentful toward me because he loves me, as his own body and as Christ loves the Church. Ephesians 5:28 and I thank You that our life is blessed with the rewards of fidelity and that _____ rejoices in me as the wife of his youth. Proverbs 5:17-18 and that he longs to kiss me because my love delights him. Song of Solomon 1:2 and that I will always satisfy him; that he is forever captivated by my love. Proverbs 5:19 I praise Your holy name that I belong to my lover and husband and that his desire is for me. Song of Solomon 7:10 and that You bless me, Lord, by surrounding me with favor, as with a shield, and give me favor in _____'s eyes above every other woman on earth. Psalm 5:12.

I praise You, Lord, that I am his wife forever by the marriage vows we made before You in righteousness, justice, unfailing love and compassion. Hosea 2:19 And that You have made us one in flesh and spirit, that You are a witness to our marriage covenant and that I am his companion and wife. I thank You that he will not break faith with me as his partner and the wife of his youth and that You will receive his offerings with pleasure. May he also guard himself and his spirit by not breaking faith with you because You hate divorce and You hate it when a man covers himself with such violence. Malachi 2:13-16

Thank You, Lord, that _____ never forgets Your teachings and that he keeps Your commands in his heart, and that Your Word is working in our marriage and he will not be deceived by the persuasive words of the adulteress who would lead him astray or be seduced by her smooth talk. Proverbs 7:21 And that wisdom enters his heart and knowledge is pleasant to his soul. I thank You that discretion protects him and that understanding guards him. Proverbs2:10-11 and I thank You, Lord, and give you all honor and glory that the gates of hell will not prevail against us, or our marriage because we are Your Church and Jesus said the powers of hell could not conquer us. Matthew 16:18

Therefore, we will inherit a double portion in our marriage as You repay and restore what the locusts were sent among us to destroy. Joel 2:25 and I praise You for giving us Your words and wisdom, and that our marriage will overcome all adversaries because the enemy cannot contradict or resist them. Luke 21:15 and for giving us everlasting joy and a double portion instead of shame, and that instead of disgrace, we will rejoice in our inheritance. Isaiah 61:7

  I praise You, Lord, that _____ will once again acknowledge You and that You won't let anyone take him out of Your hands even if You take away his prosperity and expose him and put an end to all of his celebrations because he forgot You. And I thank You, Lord, for alluring him back by leading him into the desert and speaking tenderly to him while he is there. I thank You for restoring what was lost and for transforming our valley of trouble into a gateway of hope. I give You all praise and honor that he will return to me and give himself to me as he once did, and he will call me his wife and be happy with me as before. And that he will forget all about other lovers and that their names will never again be spoken. Hosea 2:8-17

  Thank You, Father, that Jesus redeemed me from the curse of the law by being made a curse for me. Galatians 3:13. I thank You that _____ and I are reconciled to You through Jesus, by His blood shed on the cross, and that we are reconciled back to each other despite anything we've done to each other in the past. We are now presented holy before You without blemish and free from accusation through His death. Colossians 1:20-22. I give You praise and honor, Lord, that no weapon formed against our marriage has prospered, and that You are proving every voice raised against our reconciliation wrong because this is my heritage as Your child and it is Your vindication for me. Isaiah 54:17

I praise You, Lord, that Your grace is sufficient for me as I stand for the restoration of my marriage, and that Your power is made perfect in my weakness and that the power of Christ is in me. 2 Corinthians 12:9 And I am strong and courageous, not afraid or discouraged, because Your power is greater than the power of Satan and all who do his work. 2 Chronicles 32:7. I am so thankful that You are watching to make certain that Your Word is fulfilled and that You are performing it in our marriage. Jeremiah 1:12. I praise and thank You, Lord, for keeping forever the promise you have made concerning me and my home and for doing as you promised so that Your name will be great forever. O Sovereign LORD, you are God! Your words are trustworthy, and you have promised these good things to me. You have said that You will build a home for me and that it pleases You to bless my marriage so it will continue before You forever. You have spoken, and with Your blessing, my home and marriage will be established with blessings forever. AMEN. 2 Samuel 7:25-29

(www.faithandmarriageministries.org)

Spiritual Warfare Scriptures

Are you ready to do battle for your marriage or your loved one? Put on the Armor of God, and saddle up. Firmly grip the Sword of the Spirit in your hands and get ready to start swinging.

I've put together a list of my favorite spiritual warfare scriptures. I've also inserted brackets [ ] so you can insert your, or your loved one's, name as you pray. By entering the person's name, you are speaking and praying God's Word over yourself or them. This is an extremely powerful spiritual weapon against the enemy. Picture yourself with both hands on the Sword of the Spirit, which is a one-edged sword. By you speaking these scriptures out loud the sword becomes the two-edged sword, swinging from left to right and cutting down the enemy. Wow! That's powerful!

Example: "Do not fear them [son or daughter], for the Lord your God is the one fighting for you."

Old Testament Scriptures

~"Do not fear them, [ ], for the Lord your God is the one fighting for you." Deuteronomy 3:22

~"[ ], the Lord will cause your enemies who rise against you to be defeated before you. They shall come out against you one way and flee before you seven ways." Deuteronomy 28:7

~"Have I not commanded you, [ ]? Be strong and courageous! Do not tremble or be dismayed, for the Lord your God is with you wherever you go." Joshua 1:9

~"One of your men puts to flight a thousand, for the Lord your God is He who fights for you, [ ], just as He promised you." Joshua 23:10

~"This is what the Lord says to you, [ ]: 'Do not be afraid or discouraged because of this vast army. For the battle is not yours, but God's." 2 Chronicles 20:15

~"But they, [ ], who wait for the Lord shall renew their strength; they shall mount up with wings like eagles; they shall run and not be weary; they shall walk and not faint." Isaiah 40:31

~"'No weapon that is formed against you, [ ], will prosper; and every tongue that accuses you in judgment you will condemn. This is the heritage of the servants of the Lord, and their vindication is from Me,' declares the Lord." Isaiah 54:17

~"For You have girded [ ] with strength for battle; You have subdued under me those who rose up against me." Psalm 18:39

~"Through You we, [ ], will push back our adversaries, through Your name we will trample down those who rise up against us." Psalm 44:5

~"He who dwells in the shelter of the Most High will rest in the shadow of the Almighty. I, [ ], will say of the Lord,

He is my refuge and my fortress, my God, in whom I trust. Surely he will save you from the fowler's snare and from the deadly pestilence. He will cover you with his feathers, and under his wings you will find refuge; his faithfulness will be your shield and rampart..." Psalm 91:1-4

~"Not by might nor by power, but by My Spirit,' says the Lord of hosts." Zechariah 4:6

New Testament Scriptures

~"...On this rock I will build my church, and the gates of hell shall not prevail against it, [   ]." Matthew 16:18

~"Truly I tell you, [   ], whatever you bind on earth will be bound in heaven, and whatever you loose on earth will be loosed in heaven. Again, truly I tell you that if two of you on earth agree about anything they ask for, it will be done for them by my Father in heaven." Matthew 18:18-19

~"Behold, I have given you, [   ], authority to tread on serpents and scorpions, and over all the power of the enemy, and nothing shall hurt you." Luke 10:19

~"And you, [   ], will know the truth, and the truth will set you free." John 8:32

~"The thief comes only to steal and kill and destroy. I came that they, [   ], may have life and have it abundantly." John 10:10

~"I have told you these things, so that in me you, [ ], may have peace. In this world you will have trouble. But take heart! I have overcome the world." John 16:33

~"What then shall we say to these things? If God is for us, [ ], who is against us?" Romans 8:31

~"In all these things, [ ], we are more than conquerors through Him who loved us." Romans 8:37

~"[ ], Do not be overcome with evil, but overcome evil with good." Romans 12:21

"No temptation has overtaken you except what is common to mankind. And God is faithful; he will not let you be tempted beyond what you can bear. But when you are tempted, he will also provide a way out so that you can endure it." 1 Corinthians 10:13

~"But thanks be to God, who gives, [ ], us the victory through our Lord Jesus Christ." 1 Corinthians 15:57

~"For though we live in the world, we do not wage war as the world does. The weapons we fight with are not the weapons of the world. On the contrary, they have divine power to demolish strongholds. We demolish arguments and every pretension that sets itself up against the knowledge of God, and we take captive every thought to make it obedient to Christ." 2 Corinthians 10:3-5

~"[ ], Put on the full armor of God, so that you can take your stand against the devil's schemes. For our struggle is not against flesh and blood, but against the rulers, against the authorities, against the powers of this dark world and against the spiritual forces of evil in the heavenly realms. Therefore put on the full armor of God, so that when the day of evil comes, you may be able to stand your ground, and after you have done everything, to stand. Stand firm then, with the belt of truth buckled around your waist, with the breastplate of righteousness in place, and with your feet fitted with the readiness that comes from the gospel of peace. In addition to all this, take up the shield of faith, with which you can extinguish all the flaming arrows of the evil one. Take the helmet of salvation and the sword of the Spirit, which is the word of God." Epheshians 6:11-17

~"But the Lord is faithful, and he will strengthen you, [   ], and protect you from the evil one." 2 Thessalonians 3:3

~"Fight the good fight of faith, [   ]. Take hold of the eternal life to which you were called when you made your good confession in the presence of many witnesses." 1 Timothy 6:12

~"[   ], Submit yourselves to God. Resist the devil, and he will flee from you." James 4:7

~"[   ], Be self-controlled and alert. Your enemy the devil prowls around like a roaring lion looking for someone to devour. Resist him, standing firm in the faith." 1 Peter 5:8-9

"...the reason the Son of God appeared was to destroy the devil's work." 1 John 3:8

~"You are from God, little children, and have overcome them; because greater is He who is in you, [   ], than he who is in the world." 1 John 4:4

~"And they, [   ], have conquered him by the blood of the Lamb and by the word of their testimony, for they loved not their lives even unto death." Revelation 12:11

Prayer Study: When Jesus Prayed

I've included a Bible study on all the examples Jesus provided regarding prayer. Remember, prayer is a powerful weapon against the forces of evil.

- Jesus tells us to "pray without ceasing."
    - 1 Thessalonians 5:17
- Jesus prays alone:
    - Matthew 14:23
    - Mark 1:35
    - Luke 9:18
    - Luke 22:39-41
- Jesus prays in public:
    - John 11:41-42
    - John 12:27-30
- Jesus prays before meals:
    - Matthew 26:26
    - Mark 8:6
    - Luke 24:30
    - John 6:11
- Jesus prays before vital decisions:
    - Luke 6:12-13
- Jesus prays before healing:
    - Mark 7:31-37
- Jesus prays after healing:
    - Luke 5:16
- Jesus prays to do the Father's will:
    - Matthew 26:36-44
- Jesus taught on the importance of prayer:
    - Matthew 5:44
    - Matthew 6:5-15
    - Matthew 7:7-11
    - Matthew 18:19-20
    - Matthew 21:22

- Mark 11:24-26
- Luke 6:27-28
- Luke 11:9-13
- John 14:13-14
- John 15:7, 16
- John 16:23-24
- Jesus teaches how to pray "The Lord's Prayer."
  - Matthew 6:9-13
  - Luke 11:2-4
- Jesus prays to be glorified:
  - John 17.
- Jesus prays at his baptism:
- Luke 3:21-22
- Jesus prayed before traveling:
  - Mark 1:35-36
- Jesus prayed in quiet places
  - Luke 5:16
- Choosing the 12 disciples:
  - Luke 6:12-13
- Giving thanks, Jesus feeds 5000:
  - Matthew 14:19
  - Mark 6:41
  - Luke 9:16
- Giving thanks, Jesus feeds 4000:
  - Matthew 15:36
  - Mark 8:6-7
- Walking on water:
  - Matthew 14:23
  - Mark 6:46
  - John 6:15
- Healing a deaf and mute man:
  - Mark 7:31-37
- Before Peter called Jesus "the Christ."
  - Luke 9:18
- Transfiguration:
  - Luke 9:28-29
- Return of the seventy-two:

- - Luke 10:21
- Teaching His disciples, the Lord's Prayer:
  - Luke 11:1
- Raising Lazarus from the dead:
  - John 11:41-42
- Laying on hands and praying for little children:
  - Matthew 19:13-15
  - Mark 10:13-16
  - Luke 18:15-17
- Asking the Father to glorify His name:
  - John 12:27-28
- The Lord's Supper:
  - Matthew 26:26
  - Mark 14:22-23
  - Luke 22:19
- Prayed for Peter's faith when Satan asked to "sift" him:
  - Luke 22:31-32
- Prayed for Himself, His disciples, and all believers just before going to Gethsemane:
  - John 17:1-26
- In Gethsemane before His betrayal, 3 different prayers:
  1. Matthew 26:36-46
  2. Luke 22:39-46
  3. Mark 14:32-42
- After he was nailed to the cross:
  - Luke 23:34
- While dying on the cross:
  - Matthew 27:46,
  - Mark 15:34
- Jesus prayed with His dying breath:
  - Luke 23:46
- Prayed a blessing on the bread at His resurrection:
  - Luke 24:30
- He blessed the disciples before His Ascension: Luke 24:50-53
- Jesus at the right hand of the Father as an intercessor for believers:

- Roman 8:34
- Hebrew 7:25
- Hebrew 9:24
- 1 John 2:1

2=1 International

(*2=1* is the combined ministries of *Nova Shalom, Marriage Ministries International,* and *University of the Family*)

In 1983, a prophetic word was given to Mike and Marilyn Phillipps. For three years after God miraculously reconciled their marriage, they had searched for keys to complete the healing they desperately needed. A prophetic word was spoken over them of powerhouse homes, founded in the Lordship of Jesus Christ, and alive in His Kingdom principles. This was the cry of their hearts, and they longed to learn how that kind of marriage and family were created, but the man giving them the vision had no idea how it was to come about.

So, Mike and Marilyn began to study the Word of God and the Holy Spirit began teaching them key scriptures that transformed their marriage and family. They eagerly began to write down what they were learning, and soon they began sharing those lessons with other couples. By the direction of the Holy Spirit, *Married for Life* was born.

Married for Life

Married for Life is a 12-week course beginning with the covenant foundation of marriage. Coaches teach in the comfort of their own homes, and each week another Kingdom principle is taught. They bring the principles to life by living and modeling them in their own marriages. By the power of God, marriages around the world have been healed, transformed, and infused with vision and power. 2=1's goal is not just good marriages, but marriages that know what God has called them to do, and who are following that call in power and might. *Married for Life* has been planted in over 120 countries, and has been translated into 52 languages. The message contained in *Married for Life* becomes culturally relevant in every country through the examples that the coaching couples share from their own lives.

One for Life

Recognizing the need to help prepare couples for marriage, *ONE for Life* was created in 2000. It is an 8-week premarital course that, just like *Married for Life,* begins with the covenant foundation of marriage. Couples teach *ONE for Life* much the same as they do *Married for Life*. Along with teaching, they share what God has done in their own marriages and families. The scriptural principles, shared each week, focus on God's plan for marriage, family of origin/generational issues, personal healing and growth, and expectations for marriage.

Parents for Life

In 2003, *Parents for Life* was added. This 9-week course emphasizes the camaraderie of a married couple in parenting. Scriptural principles address the initial role of parenting— from conception and birth through to adulthood— and then their continuing role of influence in the family. Each week, participants are given the opportunity to look back on how they were parented, how they are currently parenting, and what they would like their parenting to look like in the future. Many couples have received healing from family of origin wounding through this course, so the outcome does not just affect the nuclear family, but produces generational healing as well.

It is estimated that over 2.7 million couples have attended *2=1* courses around the world. This year *Married for Life* is being released in video format, and it is anticipated that this will exponentially increase the number of couples reached. *2=1 International* headquarters is located in Colorado and can be reached through the website www.2equal1.com or, by direct contact at (303) 933-3331 or info@2equal1.com

About Our Ministry
~
The Marital Castle

This book in no way replaces the in-depth, small-group study that is provided through the *2=1 International* courses. Both Stephanie and I admit that, if we would have known God's desires for our marriage before getting married, we would have been so much better prepared for life. God truly had His hand upon us as we floundered down life's highway. We have both taken wrong turns on our journey, and ultimately crashed our marriage in 2016. Thanks be to God, He brought us back to life, reconciled us, and restored us as one-flesh.

If you know someone that is preparing for marriage, we invite you to please take a moment and recommend this book. It is a roadmap, showing how you and your spouse can build a Godly marital castle. We also suggest the *One for Life* course offered by *2=1 Ministries*. For this to work, both husband and wife must have a desire to align themselves with the God of Heaven, the Creator of all things.

Through *Married for Life*, we found our ministry and purpose: helping other married couples find the full potential God has had waiting for them since the beginning of time.

Has God spoken to you through *The Marital Castle*? Please bless us by sharing your testimony at our website (link below). Reach out to us and let us know how you're doing. Do you have prayer requests? Send it our way and we will gladly petition the God of the heaven on your behalf.

God has given Stephanie and I a purpose, and He wants us to tell our story. If you are interested in us coming to speak to your group, please contact us at *www.maritalcastle.com*

> *Then He Said, "Instead of shame and dishonor, you will enjoy a double share of honor. You will possess a double portion of prosperity in your land, and everlasting joy will be yours. For I, the Lord, loves justice. I hate robbery and wrongdoing. I will faithfully reward my people for their suffering and make an everlasting covenant with them."*
> *Isaiah 61:7-8 (NLT)*

Bibliography of Sources

"BibleGateway." *BibleGateway.com: A Searchable Online Bible in over 150 Versions and 50 Languages.*, www.Biblegateway.com/.

"Brain Fog Symptoms." *Mental Health Daily*, 23 Aug. 2016, mentalhealthdaily.com/2014/10/01/brain-fog-symptoms/.

"About: Church of God." *About | Church of God*, www.churchofgod.org/about/a-brief-history-of-the-church-of-god.

"Faith and Marriage Ministries." *Faith and Marriage Ministries*, www.faithandmarriageministries.org/.

"Historical Events in 1959." *OnThisDay.com*, www.onthisday.com/events/date/1959.

Hitler, Adolf. *Mein Kampf: My Struggle, Originally Entitled Four and a Half Years of Struggle against Lies, Stupidity, and Cowardice.* White Wolf, 2014.

Chapman, Gary D., and Amy Summers. *The Five Love Languages: How to Express Heartfelt Commitment to Your Mate*. LifeWay Press, 2010.

Johnson, Mary. "Breaking the Glass at Jewish Weddings." *Notes and Queries*, s9-XII, no. 293, 1903, pp. 1–116., doi:10.1093/nq/s9-xii.293.116a.

Morris, Marc. *Castles: Their History and Evolution in Medieval Britain*. Pegasus Books Ltd., 2018.

Phillipps, Mike. *Married for Life: Life-Giving Principles That Make a Marriage Last*. Eden Pub., 2012.

Spomer, Ron. *Predator Hunting: Proven Strategies That Work from East to West*. W W Norton & Co Inc, 2012.

U.S. Army Ranger Handbook. US Dept of Defense, 1985.

    Williams, Glenn F. *Dunmores War the Last Conflict of Americas Colonial Era*. Westholme, 2018.

Made in the
USA
Monee, IL